PROPOSALS FOR MONUMENTS AND BUILDINGS

Claes Oldenburg
PROPOSALS FOR MONUMENTS AND BUILDINGS
1965-69

BIG TABLE PUBLISHING COMPANY
Chicago

To Monne Ka

CONTENTS

THE POETRY OF SCALE

Oldenburg comparing a lipstick tube with the Fountain of Eros in Piccadilly Circus, London, 1966

In the following interview, Claes Oldenburg discusses the origin and development of his "Proposals for Monuments and Buildings: 1965-69." The talk was taped on August 22, 1968 in the artist's room at The Carriage House in Chicago; the interviewer is poet and editor Paul Carroll, who began by asking how the project of drawings of proposed monuments and buildings originated.

OLDENBURG:

Monuments became a significant subject for me in the spring of 1965. After a year of travel in Europe and in the U.S., away from New York, I set up in a new studio on East 14th Street. The new studio was huge—a block long—and that scale, combined with my recollections of traveling, had given me an inclination to landscape representation. I couldn't adjust this to what I'd been doing before until I hit on the idea of placing my favorite objects in a landscape—a combination of still-life and landscape scales. By rendering atmosphere and the use of perspective, I made the objects seem "colossal." Some of the first monuments were the *Vacuum Cleaner for the Battery* (Plates 1 and 2) and the *Ironing Board for the Lower East Side* (Plate 7) and the *War Memorial for Canal and Broadway* (Plate 6). The last-named metamorphosed from a pat of butter placed in the slits of a baked potato on the table where we ate. A lot of the monuments were food: pizza (Plate 5), a banana (Plate 8), a good humor bar (Plate 13), a baked potato (Plates 3 and 4), a frankfurter with tomato and toothpick (Plate 10). Then there were several versions of the *Colossal Teddy Bear* (Plate 12) sitting in the north end of Central Park or thrown there so that it rests on its side (Plate 9).

The *Teddy Bear* grew out of some hasty sketches of a huge bunny I'd done in 1958, and which could be seen as the beginning of the whole project. That year, returning from the airport, I noticed Manhattan Island from the side for the first time. I'd always thought of the island as a pile of inseparable structures — the way one sees it from the bay. But from the side, the structures detach themselves and one feels the stretch of the island — its great length. One sees a line of towers dominated by the big Empire [State Building] prick. The image of erect rabbit ears popped into my mind. "If two colossal bunny ears suddenly appeared in the Manhattan landscape," I thought, "you'd really look, wondering what in the world they were. What if you lived in Queens and, looking toward Central Park, you saw those ears? You might feel better about living in New York." The bunny was sited in the Grand Army Plaza, in front of the Plaza Hotel and by coincidence near what later became the Playboy Club. But the bunny was abandoned for another stuffed toy, the *Teddy Bear*, sited at the opposite, north end of the park.

The project began as a play with scale, and that's what it seems to be about — the poetry of scale.

The Colossal Clothespin to replace the Chicago Tribune Tower (Plate 46) is an example. When I flew to Chicago in October 1967, I took along an old-fashioned wooden clothespin because I liked its shape; I also had a postcard of the Empire State Building. I made a sketch, superimposing a clothespin on the postcard; then I stuck the clothespin in a wad of gum I was chewing, and placed it on the little table in front of my seat; and as our plane came over Chicago, I noticed that the buildings down there looked the same size as the clothespin. I made quick sketches. One showed the clothespin building (Plate 46); another, a Great Lakes ore boat in a vertical position (Plate 45); a third, smoke rising from the West Side. All three became proposals for Chicago buildings and monuments.

CARROLL:

Did you do any work on the project between 1958 and 1965?

OLDENBURG:

I made some proposals in text form—for example, the *Monument to Immigration,* proposed in 1961. Plans had been announced for the New York World's Fair, and I and some of my friends—Bob Whitman, Billy Klüver among them—felt we should try to make a big anti- or no-fair. The immigration monument was one of my contributions.

CARROLL:

Why a monument to immigration?

OLDENBURG:

Immigration has fascinated me for years—I did a Happening around 1961 called "Foto-death" which explored the theme. What occurred for most of the immigrants was a disaster: America simply wasn't what they'd expected. Well, around the same time as the World's Fair, there'd been talk about a competition for a monument to Ellis Island—the architect Philip Johnson eventually made a proposal for such a monument—and I thought I'd propose a "natural" monument in the sense it would create itself. The monument would begin as a reef placed in the bay; a ship would sail in, hit the reef, and sink; soon another would do the same; and after awhile, there'd be this big pile of wrecked, rusting ships which, as it grew, would be visible from quite a distance. The monument was inspired by a collection of World War II Liberty Ships you can see tied up on a spot up the Hudson. They're known as the "moth ball" fleet because the ships are covered by plastic cocoons. The fleet's very impressive, especially when snow covers the ships; and, in fact, the State of New York officially acknowledged that the Liberty Fleet was a monument by placing a sign and an overlook at the site. *Monument to Immigration* was my first obstacle monument. Later, I did more—such as the *War Memorial* (Plate 6) and the mini-monument *Fallen Hat (for Adlai Stevenson)* (Plate 28).

CARROLL:

Were there other influences on the project?

OLDENBURG:

There were some photos and drawings I saw in the early 1960s when I was working in the library of the Cooper Union Museum. One group of photos showed the Statue of Liberty when it first came over. Parts of the statue's body were shown lying around Madison Square: the face here, a big foot there, the hand with the torch here. I also saw some photos of those buildings in vogue around 1900 which were made to look like animals. One of these still stood in 1958, south of Atlantic City. It is the shape of an elephant, with windows, painted green and facing out to sea. Also, I came across drawings by the 18th century French architects, Boullée, Ledoux and Lequeu. A few years ago, I realized that Lequeu's building shaped like a cow was probably the model for the Teddy Bear.* Both are structures staring at you with fixed and glassy eyes.

CARROLL:

Why did you call your proposals "monuments?"

Lequeu: "Southern View of Cow's Stable on a Cool Meadow" in Visionary Architects *(University of St. Thomas, Houston, Texas, 1968, 118)*

OLDENBURG:

It was a familiar word to signify something very large. Later when I looked up the defini-tion, I realized that "monument" meant a memorial of some kind. At the beginning, I didn't think of it that way.

CARROLL:

How do you decide on the location where the monument will stand — for example, why a giant frankfurter on Ellis Island or an ironing board on the Lower East Side?

OLDENBURG:

The object is chosen because in some way it fits the shape, the conditions and the associa-tions of the site. The giant frankfurter has a shape like the ships that pass it, going up and down the Hudson. The ironing board over the Lower East echoes the shape of Manhattan island and also "shields" the vanishing ghetto, commemorating the million miles of devoted ironing. In the case of the *Teddy Bear,* an object with eyes was important. Looking up the park from the south, one casts the eyes a long distance in an area sur-prisingly empty in the midst of city congestion. The Bear's eyes are like a mirror of the huge, free glance, returning it like a tennis ball. I also imagined the staring Bear an incarnation of white conscience; as such, it fixes white New York with an accusing glance from Harlem but also one glassy-eyed from desperation. This may also be why I chose a toy with the "amputed" effect of teddy paws — handlessness signifies society's frustrating lack of tools.

15

CARROLL:

After you'd finished the first group of New York monuments in 1965, did you think about creating monuments for other cities as well?

OLDENBURG:

Not right away, or not until I began traveling again. New York was my favorite "room," my main plaything. I made toys for it, my city of cities. Then in 1966 I went to Sweden, Norway and London. In Stockholm I got a lively response to my proposals, which were presented in the papers. Swedes believe in technology. They seemed to think my monuments could actually be built someday. I presented six proposals in photo-enlargements on a billboard rented for me by the Moderna Museet in the center of town.

CARROLL:

In an interview with you in the *London International Times* (December 1966) you describe the relationship between a monument or group of them and the city in which it's to stand. What was this relationship like in Stockholm? How did it begin? And how did it evolve?

OLDENBURG:

The daily newspaper has a structure similar to the city landscape. In Stockholm, the big daily, *Svenska Dagbladet*—their *New York Times*—regularly devotes its front page to ads for nuts and bolts and other small mechanical items. All of the news appears inside the paper, after the obits—it was that way even during World War II. I was attracted particularly to the illustration of a wingnut. Comparing front page to the city landscape, I placed in the city a wingnut on an enormous scale in an appropriate site, and this became the *Wingnut Monument* (Plate 14).

The *Door Handle and Locks Monument* (Plates 15 and 16) was somewhat more complicated. This monument began as a pyramid of cannon balls seen on the island on which the Moderna Museet stands. (This island is also the former site of the Naval Establishment.) In a restaurant I'd noticed how the butter balls were served in a pyramid; and when I stuck a knife in the pyramid, I got the kind of gun-shaped angle which for some reason always makes me feel good. The gun-shape recalled the cannon. But I felt that an object more ordinary, simple and omnipresent than a cannon would be better. A few days later, I happened to be in a hardware store and I found what I wanted: a door handle with the two locks — very commonplace in Sweden. Cannon metamorphosed into Door Handle and Locks.

CARROLL:

Several monuments are very erotic — for example, the proposed Monument for Oslo-*Frozen Ejaculation (Ski Jump)* (Plate 17). How did that proposal originate?

OLDENBURG:

Do you know Frogner Park, the "Central Park" of Oslo? A famous monstrosity stands in it — some 150 monumental groups of open-air sculpture by Vigeland. He was a prodigious sculptor who'd traded his life's work to Oslo for a lifetime place in which to work, enough materials and all the necessities. Everything he created, in turn, would belong to the city and eventually be placed in Frogner Park.

One Sunday I visited Frogner Park. I was fascinated by Vigeland's huge complex: it's extremely erotic, and culminates in one gigantic shaft, which looks like a penis, composed of writing figures of men and women fighting, kissing, twisting, fucking. A Swedish critic was with me, and we'd been having some fun by wondering what could be done with the giant shaft; we made a bunch of drawings showing giants squatting on the shaft. At one point, the critic suggested hollowing out the shaft, filling it with hundreds of little, round, pink rubber babies, and then ejecting them to float like balloons all over Oslo, saturating the city. A few days later, I drew the Ski Jump. The sperm drop became a winter palace in which people skate. There is an obvious correlation between winter sports and sex: I mean, the cruelness of the knife action on ice, as well as the ski jump come.

CARROLL:

By the time you left Stockholm and Oslo and went to London, was it pretty definite that you'd continue to create monuments?

OLDENBURG:

Yes, I was aware that people were expecting me to give them a monument.

CARROLL:

Was that a good feeling, a sense of challenge — or what?

OLDENBURG:

Well, I like to work all the time; and when an artist is traveling, he has the disadvantage that he can't carry his studio along. He needs a portable kind of art, almost a literary art. To make monuments in a new city is to use that city as a studio.

CARROLL:

Would you describe in more detail how you get to know a city in which you plan to draw proposals for monuments or buildings?

OLDENBURG:

During the first two or three weeks in a new city, I try to visit as many places as possible, and be taken around by people who live there and know the city. I listen to what they say about it. Also, I try to read every newspaper and magazine on sale. I sketch a lot. And I observe the food.

Food was most influential in Sweden. When a waiter serves you, he first exhibits the plate of food as if it were sculpture or a painting; then he dishes it up and brings it back ready to eat, so you get two pictures of the dish, as if the piece were created and then taken apart and prepared for you to put in your mouth. One monument for Stockholm began with a pyramid of shrimps I'd seen in one of the restaurants. Later, the pyramid shape was tried upside-down, and helped suggest the Wingnut.

I use my body to feel and come to know a city. In London I constantly felt cold in my knees — they always ached. It was aggravated by having to squat in those small English cars. 1966 was also the time of knee exhibitionism because of the mini-skirt, especially when "framed" by boots. Oxford Street was a sea of knees.

So knees were on my mind; and since knees are doubles, I found myself collecting examples of doubles: salt and pepper shakers, double egg cups, and so on. I frequently seize on a formal idea — in this case doubles — and pursue it obsessively, collecting example after example.

I found doubles on the Thames, too. English tug boats have funnels which don't fit under bridges. Therefore, the funnels have hinges in order to fold in two when the boat sails under a bridge: so you see two funnels. I proposed two knee monuments for the Thames. One to stand at the wide part of the river, near the sea, a single knee (Plate 19); the other is the *Colossal Knees* on the Victoria Embankment, placed in that spot to echo the four chimneys of the Battersea power plant—an upended table effect, across the river. London became a sort of canvas, you see. Proposing monuments is like composing with a city. For example, in Chicago I feel the Hancock building needs something to balance it; perhaps a heavy fireplug monument at the end of Navy Pier. Restoring esthetic balance like this is an old-fashioned idea; but then, any city is an old-fashioned painting.

In London there seemed to be an obsession with water. Body moisture was agitated to the point where most people had constant colds. Ads showing people blowing their noses filled the newspapers. I proposed a *Giant Ear* to be placed in the estuary of the Thames. When the tide rose, the ear would flood; when the tide went out, the ear would empty, to be filled and then emptied by the movements of the next tide—and so on. Another water monument proposal was the *Thames Ball* (Plates 29, 30, 31).

Still another thing I noticed by being aware of my body was the London preoccupation with the throat, mouth and cigarettes. Lots of ads picture people coughing and smoking. I mated this preoccupation with the constant presence of columns and proposed the *Colossal Fag-ends for Hyde Park* (Plate 32).

CARROLL:

There seems to be a relationship between a water monument like the *Thames Ball* (Plates 29, 30, 31) which rises and sinks with the tide, and a mouth monument like the *Giant Lipstick* (Plate 18) intended to replace the Fountain of Eros in Piccadilly Circus, in that you indicate the lipstick rises out of and then sinks back into the tube.

Oldenburg comparing a mannequin's knee with a smoke stack, London, 1966

OLDENBURG:

Yes, the going in and coming out of the tide was always on my mind as I walked the streets of London. My monuments within the city are keyed to this movement, bringing the movement into the city—like breathing on a large scale. When the Thames flows out, the lipstick goes back inside the tube; when the river rises again, so does the lipstick.

And since lipstick is an ordinary object, the Giant Lipstick is a non-idealistic symbol meant to substitute for the old, idealistic symbol of love. By the way, in her note about the monuments in *Studio International,* Jasia Reichardt criticized my choice of an object because women don't use lipstick any more. What I had in mind was lipstick worn by English women in the 1940s and 50s. Do you remember the English films that came over after the war? Women in them were strange creatures with big hats, long skirts, enormous shoes, and lots and lots of lipstick. That's what I was recalling when I drew the monument. I guess I was memorializing the nostalgia which surrounds World War II.

CARROLL:

How do you feel about a possible indignant response from Londoners who might accuse you of replacing a traditionally cherished landmark like the Fountain of Eros with a vulgar pop art lipstick monument? You also propose to replace the Nelson Column in Trafalgar Square with the colossal *Gearshift in Motion* (Plate 21).

OLDENBURG:

Most of the grand sites in any city have already been taken by monuments. When I propose publicly to substitute a new monument for a landmark (as I did over the B.B.C.), it generally creates response from the citizens, but not all of it is indignant. In Stockholm it was. When I proposed placing the *Wingnut* on the site of an existing pool used by kids for wading and sailing boats, a mother sought me out to protest. In London, however, a cab driver told me he thought it was a great idea to put something more contemporary in place of monuments like Nelson Column. Not only would the Gearshift be a modern version of a column but it's also an appropriate monument because of the constant traffic congestion in Trafalgar Square. The Gearshift moves through the positions with a jolt that makes pigeons scatter in the air. I suppose the substitution of a simple industrial object for a landmark might arouse more indignation in London than in Stockholm. Industry in England is not regarded as optimistically as it is in Sweden — as if a sense of coal-colored guilt hung about the place where the Industrial Revolution originated.

CARROLL:

Have you thought about proposing a monument which might embody English guilt over the Industrial Revolution?

OLDENBURG:

No. But I have felt that the Hancock building in Chicago might be such a building — that is, at first, when I tended to get romantic about it. In its incomplete, uninhabited stage, the Hancock building reminded me of graveyard monuments. Like the visionary architecture I've mentioned, it looked awesome, strange. It followed me about.

But once I'd lived across the street from the Hancock building for a week or so, and looked at it a lot and met the architect, Bruce Graham, much of the romantic impression wore off, though I still see it as a remarkable building. When Bruce Graham took me up to the top, it reminded me of a vacant lot 100 stories high.

What really fascinates and strikes me as radical about the Hancock building is that it isn't intended to make Chicagoans feel proud by providing a symbol of the city and its culture. One hears people ask: "Why isn't the Hancock building the tallest in the world? A few more floors and it would be bigger than the Empire State building—the Second City Complex." Nor is it a monument to the architect's vision. Louis Sullivan or Frank Lloyd Wright or Mies van der Rohe made an effort to create inspiring buildings. The radical thing about the Hancock building is that it's machine-made: its height, shape, everything was determined on the basis of how the computer solved the function the building is supposed to provide in the space allotted. Take the slope of the building: it isn't the result of the architect's romantic dream or an attempt to make the structure look like an obelisk. The Hancock building looks the way it does because its shape is the most practical way the computer solved all the various problems.

CARROLL:

Does your recent interest in architecture mean that the project might be entering a new phase?

OLDENBURG:

I think so. At first, the monuments were playful, personal fantasies; then the monuments seemed to become more real and public. I remember Gene Baro, the poet, asking me in an interview we did in 1966: Did I have any idea of what type of materials would be used if one of the monuments were actually to be built? I hadn't thought too much about it. Earlier that year, three students of architecture at Cornell made an appraisal of the *War Memorial* (Plate 6). Their estimates shocked me: they figured that it would weigh 5,000,000 lbs., if concrete were used; and that the memorial would sink through the surface the way a pat of butter melts in a baked potato, crushing the subway. Then they drew up plans for rerouting the subways. It was the artist's reverie imposed on nature with a vengeance — absurd fact, the best kind of all.

I also became aware that practicing architects had taken some interest in the monuments. An invitation came from MIT to talk about projects; I felt honored but rather terrified of being caught out of my element. My monument proposals in relation to tradition began to interest me.

A friend who is a student of architecture at Yale told me that the kind of objects I choose are the closest thing to symbols available in our time. Architects find it difficult to design monuments today, he said, because they can't find appropriate symbols. Didn't Lewis Mumford say that there's no such thing as a monument in the modern world? The old symbol of the hero has disappeared. Also, architects face the problem that whatever is built today is expected to provide some practical civic service — a place to take the baby buggy. My proposals, in keeping with older traditions, do *not* provide such service.

On the contrary, many of my monuments reintroduce the idea of the monument as obstacle or disruption in the city. Many monuments, of course, are exactly that: the Arc de Triomphe, for one, is an aggressive obstacle in that traffic must be rerouted around it. So is my *War Memorial* (Plate 6): I wanted it to be like a wound in the city. Studies have indicated, in fact, that the intersection of Canal and Broadway, where the memorial would be, is the perfect spot to drop the H-bomb in order to create maximum damage and fallout throughout the New York area.

CARROLL:

Are the *Bowling Balls* (Plate 37) rolling down Park Avenue such an obstacle monument?

25

OLDENBURG:

Absolutely. The balls are an attempt to make tangible my feeling that Park Avenue is a dangerous street where you can get run over and killed very easily. The balls intensify and monumentalize this danger. Imagine you're waiting at a cross street; you want to get across Park Avenue. One ball's just rolled by; another is bearing down not too far behind it; ball after ball keeps coming: they don't respect stop lights. You must be very quick and clever if you want to get across. I feel this about New York in general. To survive you must be fast, clever, and learn the rhythm of how to walk the streets, which has nothing to do with traffic lights.

The Thames Ball is another obstacle monument; it could be a sport for ships and boats to try and dodge it.

CARROLL:

How do you feel about the recent architectural phase of the project?

OLDENBURG:

As I said, it's a bit frightening to me to be taken seriously, and I have to decide whether I really want to convert my fantasy to real projects, and on what terms this can be done. One problem is that the shape of my objects makes it harder to build them than if they had abstract forms like cubes or cones. Tony Smith, the sculptor, for example, works in simple geometric forms; the great advantage he's got is that he can enlarge the basically simple form of the cube in much the same way a building's form can be expanded and enlarged.

CARROLL:

In an interview you granted in 1966 which was published in the Austrian magazine *Bau*, you were talking about the earlier phases of the project, and you commented: "The monuments should exist in the imagination. Otherwise, people will pass by one of them and say, 'Oh, that's just a 50 foot puppy dog made of concrete.'" You imply that such monuments would have far greater reality in the imagination than in tangible reality. Apparently, you no longer feel that this applies to more recent architectural monuments or buildings?

OLDENBURG:

I was afraid that what is lyrical and believable in an imaginary form might be banal and unnecessary in fact. A 50 foot puppy dog or a 650 foot teddy bear might be merely a painful eyesore, very unpoetic.

Aside from actual construction in concrete, steel or plastics, I've also thought about realizing or materializing objects by projection. One way might be to project a picture of the object on clouds. Take the teddy bear. Get a very strong light which could project the image in a three-dimensional effect. Such a night monument would look like a giant watercolor: the lyricism could come across on an enormous scale.

Another possibility might be to create mass hallucination. I'm not exactly sure how this might be done—to hypnotize people into believing they actually saw a huge teddy bear floating in the sky at night.

CARROLL:

How does your relationship to the city and your experience of it differ in the third phase of the project as compared to how it would be if you were still working in earlier phases—throwing favorite objects on the city or being involved with factual response to imaginative projection? Do you feel a different response to the city or do you continue to read the newspapers, use your body, and so on, as you did in London?

OLDENBURG:

I go through the same preparations but now I tend to focus on the type of object that seems possible to construct. The *Windshield Wiper for Grant Park* (Plates 40, 41, 42, 43, 44) is a more architectural shape, for example, than the *Teddy Bear*. This is also true of the *Clothespin* (Plate 46).

CARROLL:

As an example of the genesis of one monument, would you describe how the *Windshield Wiper* evolved?

OLDENBURG:

The Wiper was partly suggested by the tall tapering shape of the Hancock building. If you stand in Grant Park near the Buckingham Fountain where the Wiper is sited and look at the Hancock building, it's as if you're seeing one long rectangle in perspective, which is the effect the Wiper itself would have. Here's an example of the coming together of choice of objects with a technology needed to realize it. Another source is: the Wiper defines the structure of Chicago because it's located on the Congress Expressway axis, which also happens to be the axis of Daniel Burnham's symmetrical plan for the city. Look at a map of Chicago and you'll see that the Wiper stands at the center: if you draw a compass line, it defines a semi-circular arc—the lake cuts off the circle.

CARROLL:

But why a windshield wiper?

OLDENBURG:

Chicago is a city of the meeting of water and land—a whole circle of the compass would be half water and half land. A windshield wiper occupies a place where water and "dry land" meet. In Chicago, one is always looking at the wet lake from a dry spot. And there is Burnham's concept of a facade, a "window."

Then there's the sepulchral feeling I get about Chicago, perhaps because it's so perpendicular—like tombstones. Chicago has a strange metaphysical elegance of death about it. I wanted a symbol of that: so the Grim Reaper became the Giant Wiper—a verbal play. The Wiper is as cruel as death because it comes down into the water where kids are playing. Much like the Bowling Balls careening along Park Avenue, the Wiper can "kill" kids if they don't learn how to get out of the way. Chicago seems to raise its children that way: everybody's out to get rid of the other person in this terribly competitive city.

CARROLL:

What would you say to the argument of some city booster who'd claim that a monument of a windshield wiper hardly captures Chicago as powerful, vital, masculine builder — "city of the broad shoulders," as Sandburg wrote? Or if the booster said: "Are you suggesting that we wipe or clean up the city, huh?"

OLDENBURG:

The objections would be a simple-minded explanation of what the Wiper is all about: my intentions are more poetic. For example, the Wiper also makes the sky *tangible* in that it treats the sky as if it were glass. Making the intangible tangible has always been one of my fascinations. But "wipe out" is slang for kill, isn't it? And the "Chicago typewriter," I realize, is a machine gun. Another famous Chicago typewriter is the one sunk by Leopold and Loeb in the Jackson Park Lagoon. In my *Memorial to Clarence Darrow*, a typewriter rises out of the water at the spot at certain times of day and night. It recalls an event I covered as a reporter for the City News Bureau in the early 50s. Darrow, who'd defended Leopold and Loeb, had made a "promise" to reappear after death on his birthday at the spot the typewriter was sunk. For years the papers sent reporters to the scene but Darrow never appeared.

Another funeral monument for Chicago is the *Pinetop Smith Monument:* a wire extending the length of North Avenue, west from Clark Street, along which at intervals runs an electric impulse colored blue so that there's one blue line as far as the eye can see. Pinetop Smith invented boogie woogie blues at the corner of North and Larrabee, where he finally was murdered: the electric wire is "blue" and dangerous.

CARROLL:

How would you answer a critic who pointed out that all of your memorial or sepulchral monuments — the typewriter for Clarence Darrow, the electric wire for Pinetop, the fallen hat for Adlai Stevenson — depict only objects instead of people as in such classical monuments as the statue of Moses which Michaelangelo made for the tomb of Pope Julius II?

OLDENBURG:

I guess that reflects a principle of all my work: I never show a human being or whole body; instead, I depict objects related to the person or a part of the body. You could say the spectator himself supplies the whole body in question. Usually the object is something the spectator could wear, use, eat or relate his body to.

CARROLL:

Didn't you propose a memorial monument to John F. Kennedy?

OLDENBURG:

I've proposed two monuments to Kennedy. One was a construction proposed for *Documenta* — the art exhibit held in 1968 in Kassel, Germany. I'd come to feel that the scene showing the path of the motorcade and the spot of the assassination had been photographed and dwelt on so often that it had become a monument in itself. So I wanted to literally reconstruct the scene itself — the roadway, the bridge, and the buildings — and then have a real motorcade drive through it twice a day.

CARROLL:

How would you answer criticism which might argue that such an impersonal, cold-blooded monument insults the memory of the late President?

OLDENBURG:

No insult intended. The fact is terrible enough—a more traditional monument would seem false.

CARROLL:

What is the other Kennedy memorial you mention?

OLDENBURG:

It's an underground monument (Plate 54). The corpse of the public figure is sealed in a plastic shape in the position of a well-known photograph of the subject. This shape is then suspended by a thin wire *inside* a colossal version of the same shape. The figure hangs upside-down and rotates slightly with the movement of the earth.

CARROLL:

On this visit to Chicago, you have spent two mornings and one afternoon at the Graceland Cemetery and I notice these snapshots of Lorado Taft's memorial sculpture *Statue of Death* which stands in the Cemetery. How do you propose to use this monument?

OLDENBURG:

I enlarged a photo of the sculpture and then collaged it in along North Michigan Avenue next to the Hancock building. The monument shows a figure in robes with only nose and feet visible: it would be 100 stories tall—like the Hancock building (Plate 56). I suppose I was comparing the Hancock building to the black marble slab behind the sculpture, or maybe just trying to do to the Hancock building what it has done to the Playboy building—the three of them would make a nice group.

CARROLL:

How would you reply to the question: Is this how Oldenburg sees modern American life —a world containing only the apotheosis of middle class icons: vacuum cleaner, toys, baseball bats, hats, windshield wipers on our chariot cars—and so on?

OLDENBURG:

A catalogue could be made of all such objects, which would read like a list of the deities or things on which our contemporary mythological thinking has been projected. We *do* invest religious emotion in our objects. Look at how beautifully objects are depicted in ads in Sunday newspapers. Those wonderful, detailed drawings of ironing boards, for example, showing the inside of the board flipped back to reveal how it's made: it's all very emotional. Objects are body images, after all, created by humans, filled with human emotion, objects of worship.

However, the idea of an object as a magic thing no longer obsesses me as it once did. In the Clothespin building, for example, I guess the object was originally a magic thing to me —like a rabbit's foot or bone or relic—but I became far more interested in the architectural form of the clothespin, which seemed somewhat gothic to me, like the Tribune Tower itself.

When you think about the project as it's grown from phase to phase, in fact, it almost looks like growing up from a child's fantasy.

CARROLL:

Do you suggest something like this: The earliest phase was much like tiny Gulliver among the Brobdingnagians and their giant objects—ironing board, vacuum cleaner, toilet float? Toys, too, of course, like the teddy bear.(The magical reality you invest in such objects reminds me of di Chirico's painting *Playtoys of the Prince.)*Then there's the pubescent phase. Not only are its objects sexual—such as *Ski Jump* sperm—but they're mechanical. Most teenage boys like to fool around with wing nuts, locks, and so on. The current phase, then, is "adult" in the sense it's like building in the real world.

OLDENBURG:

I find that a pleasing explanation; but remember, I haven't yet managed to construct anything on the scale of the proposals. The fantasy of scale has not succumbed to reality.

CARROLL:

When will your project be finished? Do you ever feel that you may have created a Frankenstein monster in the sense that you may have to visit every city in the world, including Rangoon, before the project is finished?

OLDENBURG:

I'm not interested in just going from city to city knocking out monument proposals. Recently, some collectors invited me to visit new cities and create monument fantasies but I had to say "No."I wanted to concentrate on the possibility of actually getting something constructed.

New York, Chicago and Los Angeles are the American cities I prefer to use because they seem like such typical cities. Going to Seattle or New Orleans or wherever would seem beside the point. If I went to the Orient, I probably would choose to visit what I considered typical cities there—Calcutta, for example.

CARROLL:

Are the monuments you've made for Los Angeles part of your current architectural phase?

OLDENBURG:

Some of them. I proposed an alternative design for the new Pasadena Art Museum based on an advertisement showing an open package of cigarettes against half of a tobacco tin. (Plate 52). It didn't seem far-fetched. In an enlarged version, the package and tin are very building-like and even adapt well to the different functions: a library and restaurant in the extended cigarettes; the exhibits in the package itself; the auditorium in the half tin. From the ground, the structure would appear abstract; it would only look like the original from the air.

The many letter-forms silhouetted against the sky in the Los Angeles basin led to the proposal of colassal block letters scattered across the countryside. These are simple and architectural and, at close hand, also abstract. I further suggested making buildings out of the letters of the word that describes the building's function. A bank, for example, using B-A-N-K in colossal form, or P-O-L-I-C-E for a police headquarters (Plate 51). Arguments about how a building should look would be reduced to arranging these huge letters. Such structures would blend well with those existing in Los Angeles.

The construction of tunnel entrances on the Los Angeles freeway in the form of noses

(Plate 53) recalls the more organic subjects but there is a new element of practicality—the use of a sloping hill for support, for example, and the low profile. The nose entrances could easily be built if the citizens wanted them.

CARROLL:

From what you've been saying, it looks as if your project will continue to evolve. Will you explore it until it's finished?

OLDENBURG:

Certainly. I'd finish it today if I could but I know it's not done yet. Anyway—it's been interesting to have entered the world through the door of a little impressionist watercolor. I wonder where it will end.

Oldenburg London, 1966

PLATE SECTION

Plate 1

Artist's Catalogue: Monuments/1

Proposed Colossal Monument for the Battery, NYC: Vacuum Cleaner (View from the Upper Bay). 1965.
Crayon and watercolor. 23 × 29 inches

Collection Jonathon D. Scull, New York.

N.41

C.d.6'

Plate 2

Artist's Catalogue: Monuments/2

Proposed Colossal Monument for the Battery, NYC: Vacuum Cleaner (East River View). 1965.
Crayon and watercolor. 12 × 17¾ inches.

Collection Mrs. Robert M. Benjamin, New York.

Plate 3
Artist's Catalogue: Monuments/4

Proposed Colossal Monument for Grand Army Plaza, NYC: Baked Potato. 1965.
Crayon and watercolor. 18 × 21½ inches.

Collection Mr. and Mrs. Ira Licht, New York.

44

B. P. in
Grand Plaza

Plate 4

Artist's Catalogue: Monuments/5

Proposed Colossal Monument for Grand Army Plaza, NYC: Baked Potato (Thrown Version). 1965.
Crayon and watercolor. 23 × 29 inches.

The Baltimore Museum of Art, Thomas E. Benesch Memorial Collection.

Plate 5

Artist's Catalogue: Monuments/7

Proposed Colossal Monument for New York Harbor: Pizza for Upper Bay. 1965.
Crayon and watercolor. 11¾ × 17½ inches.

Mr. and Mrs. Edwin A. Bergman, Chicago, Illinois.

from New York Harbor   CO 7/66

Plate 6

Artist's Catalogue: Monuments/9

Proposed Monument for the Intersection of Canal Street and Broadway, NYC:
Block of Concrete, Inscribed with the Names of War Heroes. 1965.
Crayon and watercolor. 11¾ × 17½ inches.

Mr. and Mrs. Daniel N. Flavin, Jr., Cold Spring, New York.

Bény — Canal St. Martin —

Plate 7

Artist's Catalogue: Monuments/10

Proposed Colossal Monument for Lower East Side, NYC: Ironing Board. 1965.
Crayon and watercolor. 21¾ × 29½ inches.

Collection of Mr. and Mrs. Marvin Goodman, Toronto, Canada.

52

n.y.   C.Ive 1965

Plate 8

Proposed Colossal Monument for Times Square, NYC: Banana. 1965.
Crayon and watercolor. 11½ × 17½ inches.

Collection Mr. and Mrs. Richard L. Selle, Chicago, Illinois.

54

Banana

Plate 9

Artist's Catalogue: Monuments/19

Proposed Colossal Monument for New York Park: Teddy Bear (Thrown Version).
1965.
Crayon and watercolor. 23 × 29 inches.

The Collection of Alfred Heller, Grass Valley, California.

Plate 10

Artist's Catalogue: Monuments/25

Proposed Colossal Monument for Ellis Island: Frankfurter with Tomato and Toothpick. 1965.
Crayon and watercolor. 22 × 30 inches.

Collection of Mr. and Mrs. Michael Blankfort, Los Angeles, California.

C.D. 65

Plate 11

Artist's Catalogue: Monuments/26

Proposed Colossal Monument for Ellis Island: Shrimp. 1965.
Crayon and watercolor. 12 × 15½ inches.

The Collection of Mr. and Mrs. Dirk Lohan, Chicago, Illinois.

Plate 12

Artist's Catalogue: Monuments/28

Proposed Colossal Monument for Central Park North, NYC: Teddy Bear. 1965.
Crayon and watercolor. 23 × 19 inches.

Collection of Mr. and Mrs. Richard E. Oldenburg, New York.

Plate 13

Artist's Catalogue: Monuments/31

Proposed Colossal Monument for Park Avenue, NYC: Good Humor Bar. 1965.
Crayon and watercolor. 23½ × 17½ inches.

Collection Carroll Janis, New York.

Plate 14

Artist's Catalogue: Monuments/34

Proposed Monument for Karlaplan, Stockholm: Turning Wingnut. 1966.
Photoprint from pencil. 11⅝ × 16½ inches.

Collection the Artist, New York.

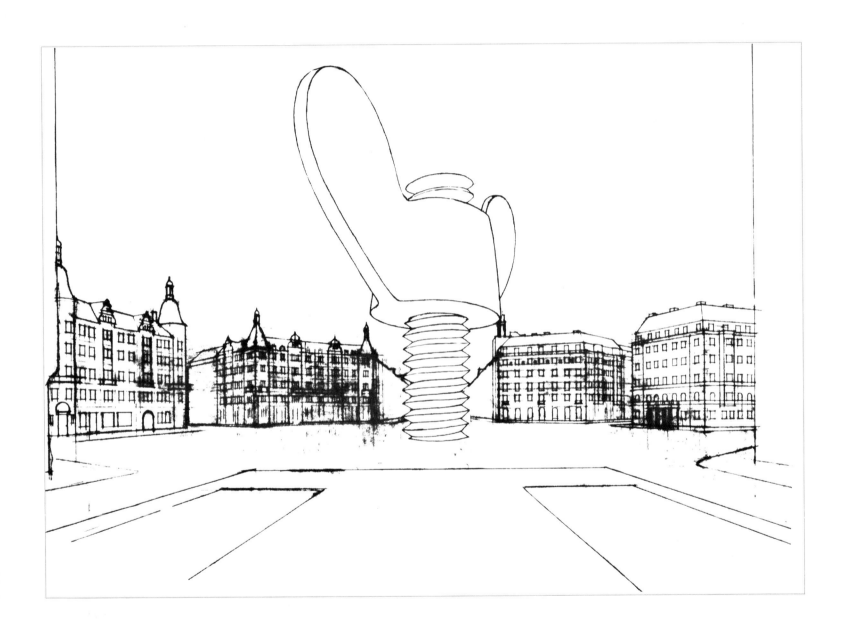

Proposed Colossal Monument Behind the Moderna Museet, Stockholm: Swedish Doorhandle and Locks (Two Views). 1966.
Pencil. 11⅝ × 16½ inches; 11¼ × 16½ inches.

Collection the Artist, New York.

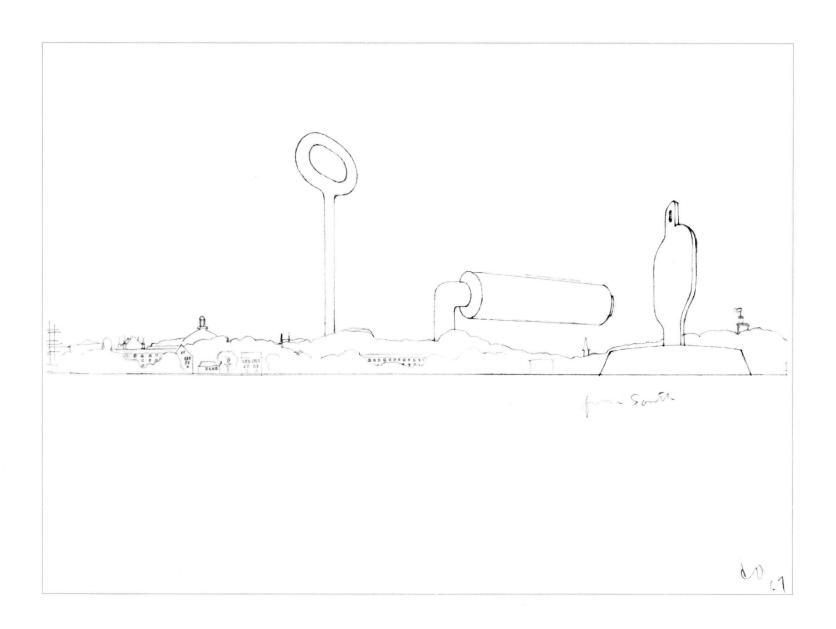

from South

Plate 16

Artist's Catalogue: Monuments/35

Proposed Colossal Monument Behind the Moderna Museet, Stockholm: Swedish Doorhandle and Locks (Two Views). 1966.
Pencil. 11⅝ × 16½ inches; 11¼ × 16½ inches.

Collection the Artist, New York.

70

Plate 17

Artist's Catalogue: Monuments/54

Proposed Monument for Oslo: Frozen Ejaculation (Ski Jump). 1966.
Crayon and watercolor. 22 × 30 inches.

The Collection of Mr. and Mrs. Dirk Lohan, Chicago, Illinois.

72

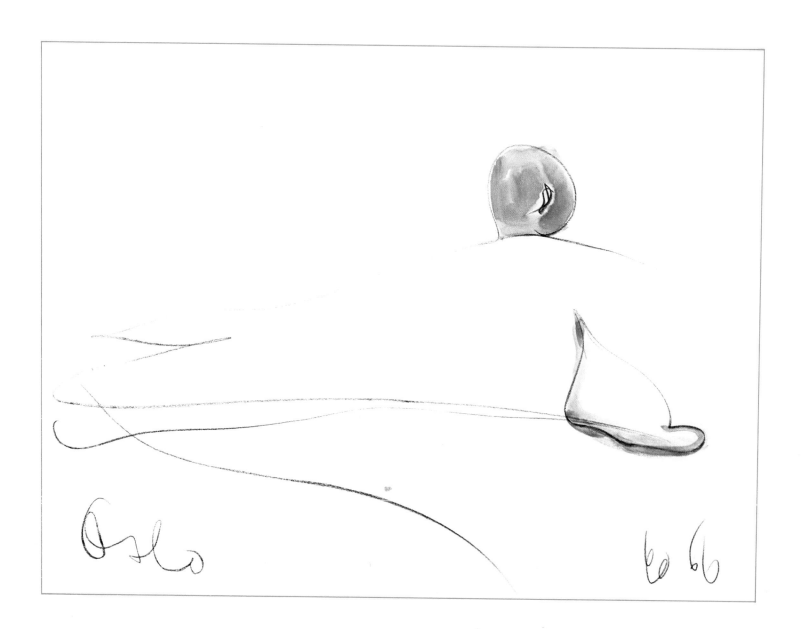

Plate 18

Artist's Catalogue: Monuments/40

Various Positions of a Giant Lipstick to Replace the Fountain of Eros, Piccadilly Circus. 1966.
Crayon and watercolor. 18 × 24 inches.

John and Kimiko Powers, Aspen, Colorado.

1   2   3   4   5

Plate 19

Artist's Catalogue: Monuments/42

Proposed Colossal Monument for Thames Estuary: Knee. 1966.
Crayon and watercolor. 15¼ × 22⅛ inches.

D. and J. de Menil Collection, Houston, Texas.

Plate 20

Artist's Catalogue: Monuments/43

Proposed Colossal Monument for Thames Estuary: Knee. 1966.
Crayon and watercolor. 15 × 22 inches.

The Collection of Mr. and Mrs. Dirk Lohan, Chicago, Illinois.

78

Plate 21

Artist's Catalogue: Monuments/45

Proposed Colossal Monument to Replace the Nelson Column in Trafalgar Square:
Gearstick in Motion. 1966.
Crayon and watercolor. 19 × 26 inches.

Private Collection, New York.

Plate 22

Artist's Catalogue: Monuments/47

Proposed Colossal Monument for Thames River: Thames Ball (View from Below).
1966.
Crayon and watercolor. 15 × 22 inches.

Collection Neil A. Levine, New Haven, Connecticut.

Thamesball

Plate 23

Artist's Catalogue: Monuments/49

Proposed Colossal Monument for Battersea Park: Drum Set. 1966.
Crayon and watercolor. 15 × 22 inches.

Mr. and Mrs. Edwin A. Bergman, Chicago, Illinois.

Plate 24

Artist's Catalogue: Monuments/50

Fixture for a London Taxi: Interior Lamp in the Form of an Ear. 1966.
Crayon and watercolor. 21½ × 14½ inches.

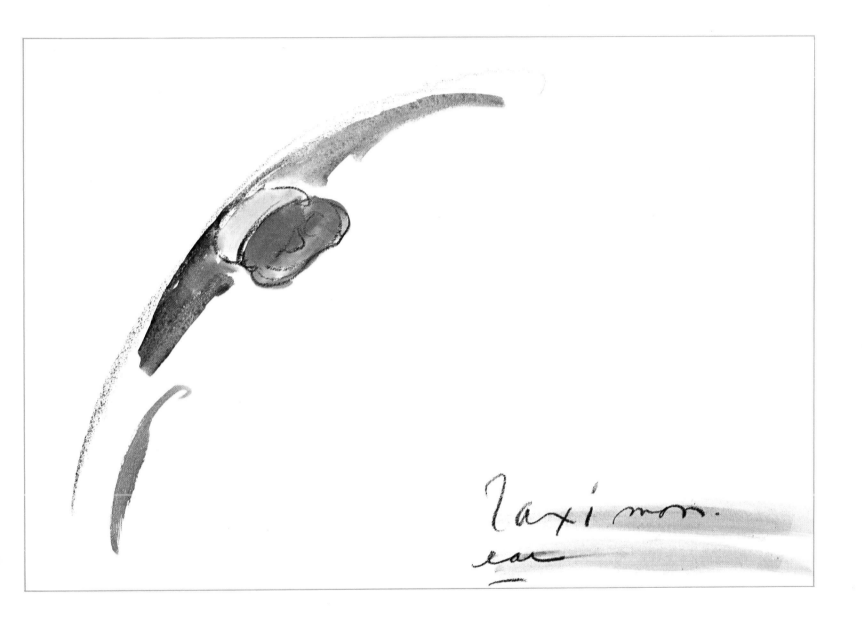

Plate 25

Artist's Catalogue: Monuments/57

Proposed Colossal Monument for Toronto: Drainpipe. 1967.
Pencil and watercolor. 23 × 30 inches.

Private Collection, Houston, Texas.

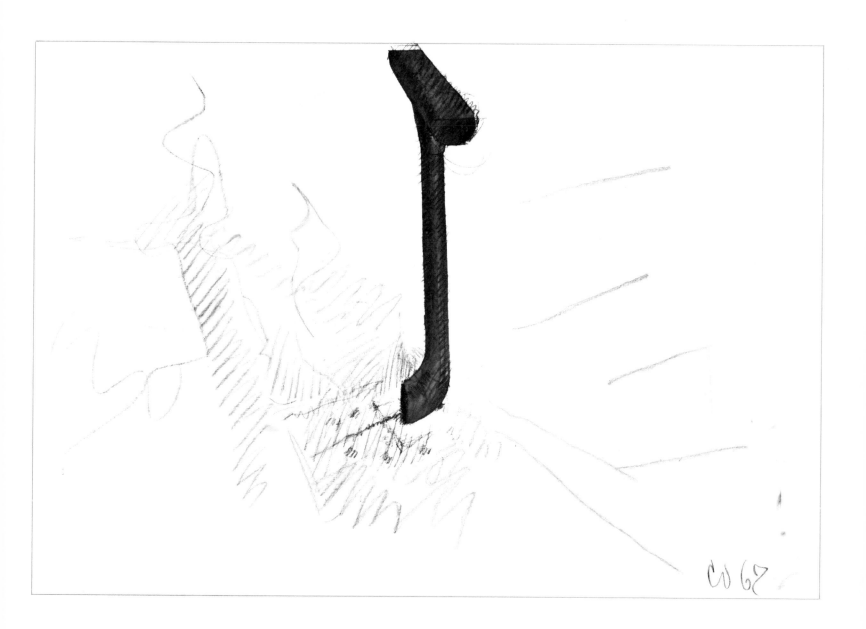

CU 68

Plate 26

Artist's Catalogue: Monuments/60

Base of Colossal Drainpipe Monument, Toronto, With Waterfall. 1967.
Pencil and watercolor. 24¾ × 22 inches.

John and Kimiko Powers, Aspen, Colorado.

Plate 27 ·

Artist's Catalogue: Monuments/61

Base of Colossal Drainpipe Monument, Toronto (Front View). 1967.
Ink and watercolor. 11 × 8½ inches.

Collection of Mr. and Mrs. Michael Blankfort, Los Angeles, California.

Plate 28

Artist's Catalogue: Monuments/66

Small Monument for a London Street: Fallen Hat (For Adlai Stevenson). 1967.
Pencil and watercolor. 23 × 32 inches.

John and Kimiko Powers, Aspen, Colorado.

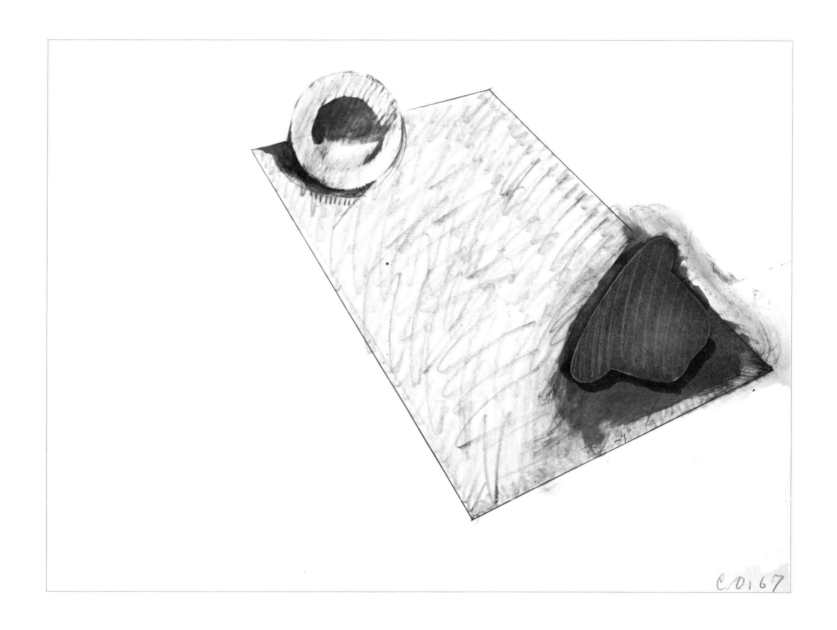

CD 67

Plate 29

Artist's Catalogue: Monuments/67

Proposed Colossal Monument for Thames River: Thames Ball. 1967.
Crayon, pen and watercolor on postcard. 3½ × 5½ inches.

Collection of Edwin Janss, Thousand Oaks, California.

Plate 30

Artist's Catalogue: Monuments/68

Proposed Colossal Monument for Thames River: Thames Ball. 1967.
Crayon, pen and watercolor on postcard. $3\frac{1}{2} \times 5\frac{1}{2}$ inches.

Collection Carroll Janis, New York.

98

Plate 31

Artist's Catalogue: Monuments/69

Proposed Colossal Monument for Thames River: Thames Ball (View From River).
1967.
Pencil and watercolor. 26¼ × 40 inches.

Collection Mr. and Mrs. Richard H. Waddell, New York.

Plate 32

Artist's Catalogue: Monuments/52

Study for Colossal Monument: Fagends (in Hyde Park). 1966.
Crayon and watercolor. 15 × 22 inches.

Gordon Locksley Gallery, Minneapolis, Minnesota.

Plate 33

Artist's Catalogue: Monuments/51

Small Study for Colossal Monument: Fagend. 1966.
Crayon and watercolor. 7 × 9¾ inches.

Collection Mr. and Dr. Ivan C. Karp, New York.

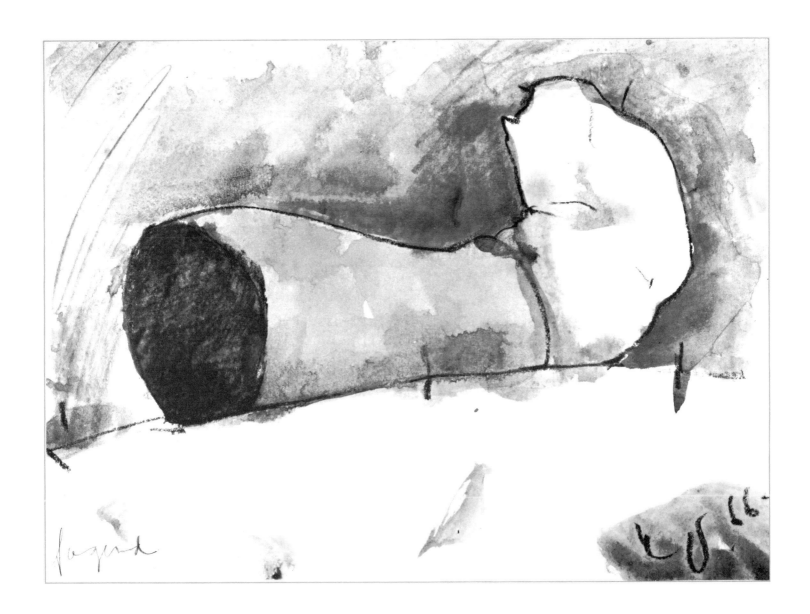

Plate 34

Artist's Catalogue: Buildings/2

Beach House for East Hampton, Long Island, in the Form of a Doorhandle. 1967.
Pencil. 22 × 30 inches.

Plate 35

Artist's Catalogue: Monuments/70

Proposed Colossal Monument: Fan in Place of the Statue of Liberty. 1967.
Pencil. 26 × 40 inches.

Collection of Ondine Vaughn and Steve Schapiro, New York.

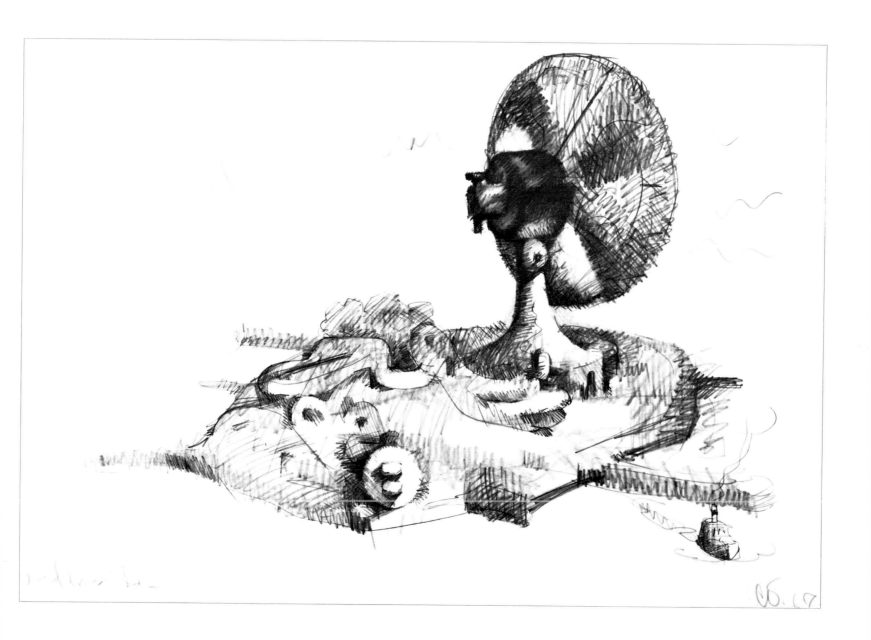

Plate 36

Artist's Catalogue: Monuments/71

Proposed Colossal Monument for Central Park, NYC: Moving Pool Balls. 1967.
Pencil and watercolor. 22 × 30 inches.

D. and J. de Menil Collection, Houston, Texas.

Plate 37

Artist's Catalogue: Monuments/72

Proposed Colossal Monument for Park Avenue, NYC: Bowling Balls. 1967.
Pencil and watercolor. 27$\frac{7}{8}$ × 22$\frac{1}{4}$ inches.

D. and J. de Menil Collection, Houston, Texas.

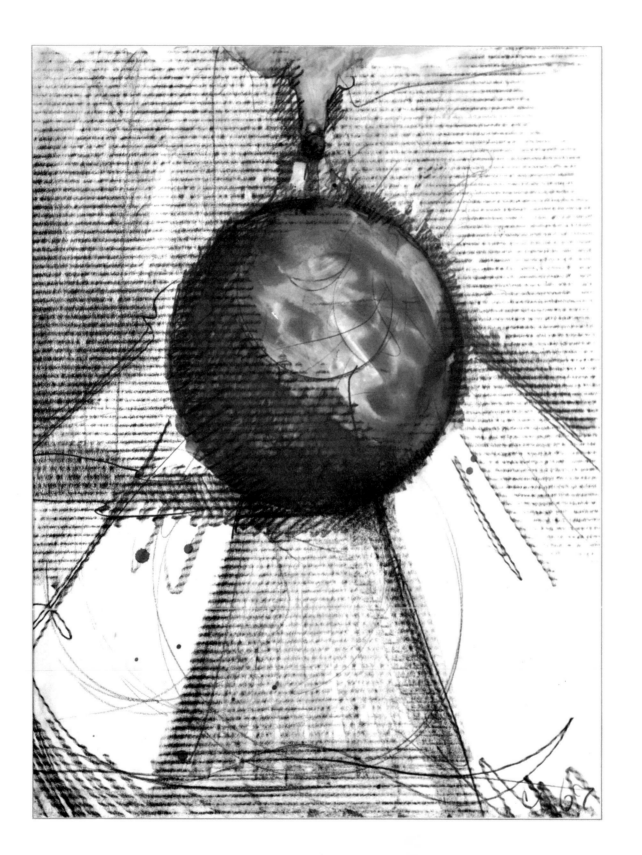

Plate 38

Artist's Catalogue: Buildings/3

Building in the Form of an English Extension Plug. 1967.
Pencil. 22 × 30 inches.

The Collection of Mr. and Mrs. Arthur I. Cohen, New York.

Plate 39

Artist's Catalogue: Buildings/4

Proposed Chapel in the Form of Swedish Extension Plug. 1967.
Crayon and watercolor. 22 × 30 inches.

Collection Krannert Art Museum, University of Illinois, Champaign.

Plate 40

Proposed Colossal Monument for Grant Park, Chicago: Windshield Wiper. 1967.
Crayon on postcards (3). Each $3\frac{1}{2} \times 5\frac{1}{2}$ inches.

Collection the Artist, New York.

Plate 41

Artist's Catalogue: Monuments/77

Proposed Colossal Monument for Grant Park, Chicago: Windshield Wiper. 1967.
Crayon on postcards (3). Each $3\frac{1}{2} \times 5\frac{1}{2}$ inches.

Collection the Artist, New York.

Plate 42

Artist's Catalogue: Monuments/77

Proposed Colossal Monument for Grant Park, Chicago: Windshield Wiper. 1967.
Crayon on postcards (3). Each 3½ × 5½ inches.

Collection the Artist, New York.

Plate 43

Artist's Catalogue: Monuments/78

Proposed Colossal Monument for Grant Park, Chicago: Windshield Wiper (Overhead View). 1967.
Crayon and watercolor. 17 × 12½ inches.

Collection Louise Ferrari, Houston, Texas.

Plate 44

Artist's Catalogue: Monuments/79

Proposed Colossal Monument for Grant Park, Chicago: Windshield Wiper
(View From Lake). 1967.
Crayon and watercolor. 14 × 17 inches.

Collection Mr. and Mrs. Richard L. Selle, Chicago, Illinois.

Plate 45

Artist's Catalogue: Buildings/5

Late Submission to the Chicago Tribune Architectural Competition of 1922:
Perpendicular Ore Boat. 1967.
Crayon and watercolor. 9¾ × 7 inches.

Private Collection, Houston, Texas.

Plate 46

Artist's Catalogue: Buildings/7

Late Submission to the Chicago Tribune Architectural Competition of 1922: Clothespin (Version Two). 1967.
Pencil, crayon and watercolor. 22 × 23¼ inches.

The Collection of Charles Cowles, New York.

Plate 47

Artist's Catalogue: Monuments/81

Proposed Monument for the South-East Corner of North Avenue and Clark Street, Chicago: Bat Spinning at the Speed of Light. 1967.
Crayon and watercolor. 17¾ × 12 inches.

Collection Frances and Sydney Lewis, Richmond, Virginia.

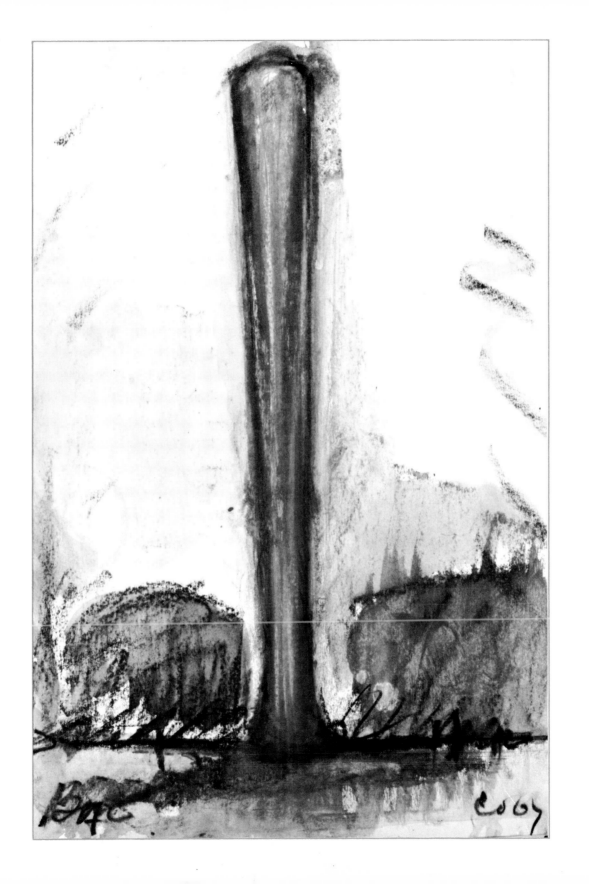

Plate 48

Artist's Catalogue: Monuments/85

Proposed Colossal Monument to Replace the Washington Obelisk, Washington, D.C.: Scissors in Motion. 1967.
Crayon and watercolor. 30 × 19¾ inches.

From the Collection of Philip Johnson, New Canaan, Connecticut.

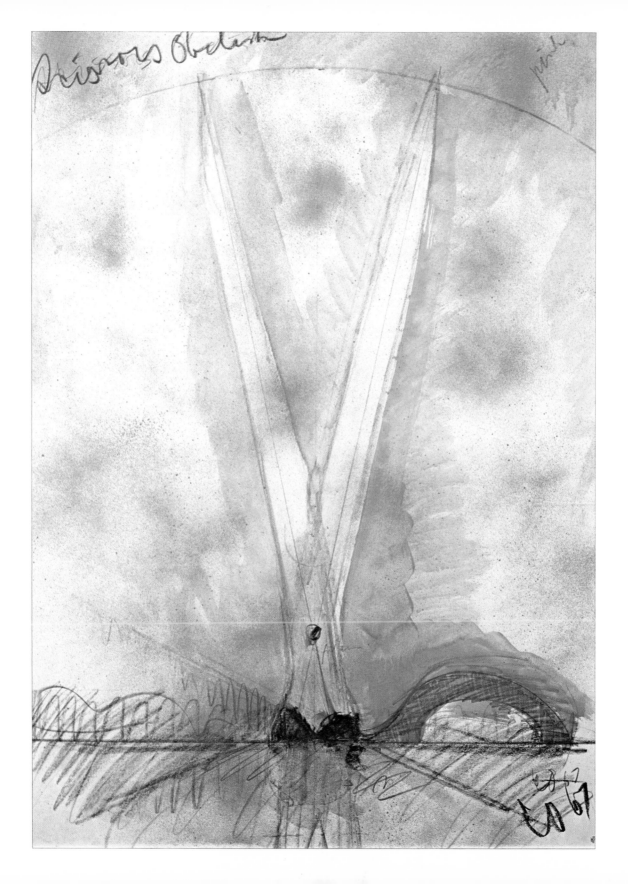

Plate 49

Artist's Catalogue: Monuments/86

The Letter Q in Landscape. 1968.
Crayon and watercolor. 10½ × 13½ inches.

The Collection of Miss Caroline F. Solovei, New York.

Plate 50

Artist's Catalogue: Monuments/87

The Letters L and O in Landscape. 1968.
Crayon and watercolor. 9½ × 13½ inches.

John and Kimiko Powers, Aspen, Colorado.

Plate 51

Artist's Catalogue: Buildings/8

Design for a Police Building Using the Word POLICE. 1968.
Pencil. 22 × 30 inches.

John and Kimiko Powers, Aspen, Colorado.

Police   CO 68

Plate 52

Artist's Catalogue: Buildings/9

Museum Design Based on a Cigarette Package. 1968.
Pencil. 22 × 30 inches.

Irving Blum Gallery, Los Angeles, California.

142

Museum   CO 68

Plate 53

Artist's Catalogue: Buildings/11

Design for a Tunnel Entrance in the Form of a Nose. 1968.
Crayon. 22 × 30 inches.

Irving Blum Gallery, Los Angeles, California.

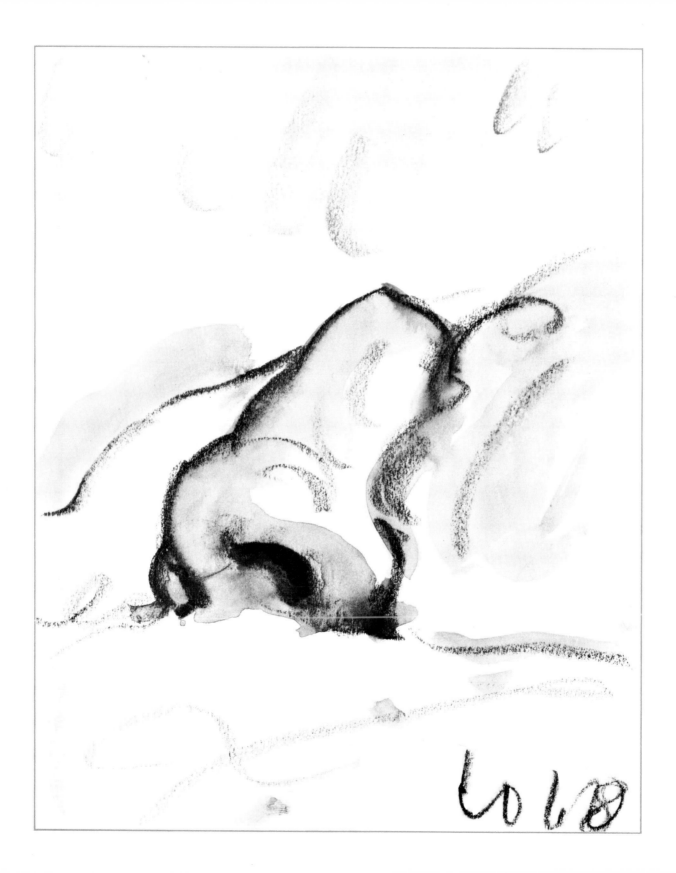

Plate 54

Artist's Catalogue: Monuments/33

Proposed Underground Memorial and Tomb for President John F. Kennedy. 1965.
Spray paint on paper cut-out. 13¾ × 11 inches.

Collection the Artist, New York.

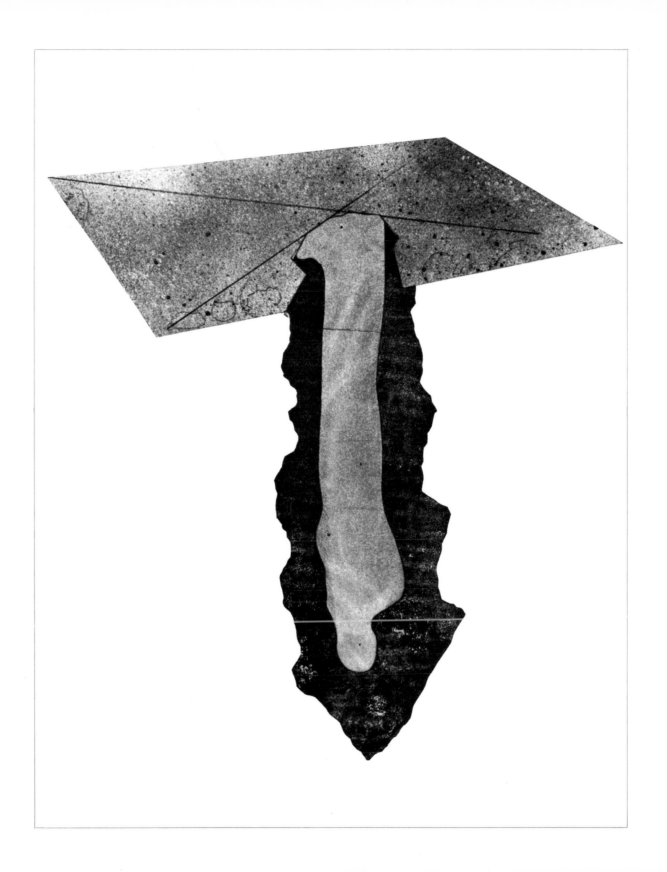

Plate 55

Artist's Catalogue: Monuments/90

Proposed Colossal Monument for the End of Navy Pier, Chicago: Fireplug (Two Views). 1968.
Pencil. 30 × 22 inches.

Plate 56

Artist's Catalogue: Buildings/18

Proposal for a Skyscraper for Michigan Avenue, Chicago, in the Form of Lorado Taft's Sculpture, "Death." 1968.
Pen and pencil on postcard and clipping. 11¾ × 9¾ inches.

Collection the Artist, New York.

1   2   3

CN 68

NOTES BY THE ARTIST ON SELECTED DRAWINGS

Oldenburg carrying his sculpture "Tube" (1964) down Oxford Street, London, 1966

The first number refers to the plate number of the drawing in this book; the second number, in brackets, to the number assigned to the drawing as listed in the complete catalogue of "Proposals for Monuments and Buildings" which begins on page 179. In those instances in which the artist's note refers to a drawing not reproduced in this book, only the catalogue number is listed. Parts of these notes originally appeared in Chelsea *#22-23 (1968) and are reprinted with permission of the editor; the note on the Windshield Wiper appeared in* Panorama, *July 22, 1967, and is reprinted with permission of* The Chicago Daily News.

If I think of my eyes as the view from an airplane, and of the floor of my studio as a landscape, then the ordinary objects lying around seem "colossal." If I then identify the landscape of the floor, as for example, Manhattan Island, the "colossal" objects acquire a specific, comparative size: a pencil sharpener the size of a five story tenement; a bed half the size of Central Park. In drawing, I sometimes feel like a worker on a huge form, a painter on an Ocean Liner. No matter what my size is, the pencil point—something so small it almost can't be seen—is the agent. Suppose the point of the pencil a human worker—a Gutzon Borglum with his chisel.

Plates 1 and 2 (Monuments/1 and 2)
Proposed Colossal Monument for the Battery, NYC: Vacuum Cleaner (1965).

Several of the first monuments were in two versions: fallen and erect.

155

Plate 4 (Monuments/5)

Proposed Colossal Monument for Grand Army Plaza, NYC: Baked Potato (1965).

The crushed potato is constructed against the wall of the Plaza Hotel as if it had been thrown there.

Plate 7 (Monuments/10)

Proposed Colossal Monument for the Lower East Side, NYC: Ironing Board (1965).

The top of the board serves as a landing place for helicopters. Passengers and visitors eat at the restaurant hung under the board, recalling the cabin of a zeppelin. They descend by diagonal elevators through the "legs."

Plate 13 (Monuments/31)

Proposed Colossal Monument for Park Avenue, NYC: Good Humor Bar (1965).

Traffic is routed through the "bite" in the bar. The monument could be constructed as a sheath over the existing Pan Am building.

Plate 14 (Monuments/34)

Proposed Monument for Karlaplan, Stockholm: Turning Wingnut (1966).

The Wingnut rises and descends on its screw in the course of a day. It is located at the most hub-like spot on the Stockholm map, at the meeting of eight streets.

Plates 15 and 16 (Monuments/35)

*Proposed Colossal Monument behind the Moderna Museet, Stockholm: Swedish Door-
handle and Locks* (1966).

The "handle" will turn in its arc; the keys will flip in their locks with a crack that can be
heard for miles. One source of the monument was the mechanical mobile by Alexander
Calder which has been reconstructed in front of the Moderna Museet—originally intended for the New York World's Fair of 1939.

Plate 17 (Monuments/54)

Proposed Monument for Oslo: Frozen Ejaculation (Ski Jump) (1966).

Constructed on a hill outside of the city and visible from the Vigeland Monument. On top
of this hill at the present time is a ski-jump. The Oslo monument replaces that with the
saucer-shaped front of a penis set on end like a radar receiver. In the center is an oval hole
through which the sky is visible and at the bottom of the hill an enormous tear-shaped
form, so large that when you are close to it you have no idea of what it might be. At a
distance, say from the position of the drawing, it would seem to be a drop of sperm at the
bottom of the hill. The drop is made of glass. Inside the drop there are skating tourna-
ments, etc.

Plate 18 (Monuments/40)

Various Positions of a Giant Lipstick to Replace the Fountain of Eros in Piccadilly Circus, London (1966).

The color red is prominent in London: the buses are very red; the cars in the tube (or subway) are red. The diagrams of the tubes under construction (posted everywhere) are also red. Red is not a very prominent color in New York where the colors tend to be black, grey, green. This presence of red worked its way into the Drainpipe (Plates 25, 26, 27). I rarely use red. These things are related: the lipstick, the drainpipe, the drawings of the tube system.

No Plate (Monuments/53)

Proposed Colossal Monument, Victoria Embankment, London: Knees (1966).

As I was flying into London, I saw a pair of kilns—two columns broader at the bottoms. They are a transition between the Swedish Light Switches and the Knees of London. The Knees Monument stands on the edge of the river; it would be very high, higher than Saint Paul's Cathedral, and it would be interesting to see the effect of the sun on it—the different colors. One could tell time by the knees.

Plate 21 (Monuments/45)

Proposed Colossal Monument to Replace the Nelson Column in Trafalgar Square, London: Gearstick in Motion (1966).

Using four positions, the Gearstick could be programmed to shift each quarter hour.

Plate 23 (Monuments/49)
Proposed Colossal Monument for Battersea Park, London: Drum Set (1966).

The drum set is intended as a pleasure palace. The drums serve as auditoriums, the cymbals as vast sloping observation roofs.

Plate 24 (Monuments/50)
Fixture for a London Taxi: Interior Lamp in the Form of an Ear (1966).

I was interested in ears, and in Stockholm part of a film we made showed Pat [Mrs. Claes Oldenburg] manipulating my ear. She had a caress for my ear in Stockholm that she did not use in London or New York. My interest in making a very small, intimate monument for London led me to imagine a monument inside a taxi cab, where you spend so much of your time in London. There is an oval light to your left above the door and that would seem to be a good spot for the substitution of a plastic ear, reddish, which could be rubbed from time to time and which would light up.

Plates 25, 26, 27 (Monuments/57, 60, 61)
Proposed Colossal Monument for Toronto: Drainpipe (1967).

When we went to Toronto in January 1967, I sketched the Drainpipe in a waterfront situation that had suggested itself as we were flying in. Coronation Park, I later gathered from the map. The monument has taken a civic center turn. It would have a waterfall in the front. There would be water inside the Drainpipe like in the submarine tower in New London, Connecticut. I also envisage a plastic top in the Drainpipe where helicopters will land; and underneath that, a giant swimming pool which might have a plastic bottom so that people could look down at Toronto from under water 850 feet *up*. At the base of the Drainpipe are two semi-circular structures used for civic events and conventions. On top, these structures form a B-shaped piazza around the base of the pipe which people can use for strolling and watching the waterfall.

The original drainpipe comes from an advertisement in a Stockholm paper which struck me because it was a picture of a hard object—a drainpipe—in a soft twisting way. I later discovered that this representation of a drainpipe—in a "T" shape with a twisting stem—was the trademark of drainpipe specialists in the city. At that time I was working on a frontispiece drawing for the catalog of a show in Toronto, and the "T" of Toronto appealed to me, perhaps because my middle name begins with "T." In many of my pieces, I incorporate the initials "C" and "O" but less frequently the "T." I thought I would start using the "T" to see what kind of luck that would bring me. One concern fit the other—"T" melted into drainpipe, and later, on a visit to Toronto, issued as a monument for the city.

Plate 28 (Monuments/66)
Small Monument for a London Street: Fallen Hat (for Adlai Stevenson) (1967).

A mini-monument. It would be a small obstacle on the street. The first thought was a shoe; the second was a pigeon, which would add an element of surprise—you would

160

approach the pigeon and expect it to fly away, and of course it wouldn't and you would fall on your face. This led into the modest monument for Stevenson who fell near Grosvenor Square. The London streets have 24-inch long rectangle stones. The fallen hat is set in such a rectangle. It could be a modest monument for anyone who died on the street. An inconspicuous monument: passersby not watching where they are going might trip on it. I was thinking of a very good friend, an older man, who had died earlier in 1966. He went out for a walk as he always did in the evening and he had a heart attack and died on the street.

Plates 29, 30, 31 (Monuments/67, 68, 69)
Proposed Colossal Monument for Thames River, London: Thames Ball (1967).

The Thames Ball is a giant copper ball—highly reflective copper, if possible—based on the form of a toilet float which is connected by a long rod to the center of one of the bridges in the Thames. It would be anchored but with a certain amount of sway. It may be that the ball will not sink down enough at low tide to make the up and down movement significant, in which case a deflatable bottom could be constructed—or the ball could look like a ball but have a flat bottom.

Plate 34 (Buildings/2)
Beach House for East Hampton, Long Island in the Form of a Doorhandle (1967).

A friend bought some property in East Hampton, Long Island, and told me that the only new structure not prohibited is a tower. The Doorhandle pivots on its base. If a lens were installed in the end of the handle, the inhabitants might relax in the living room and watch events far out at sea.

Plate 35 (Monuments/70)
Proposed Colossal Monument: Fan in Place of the Statue of Liberty (1967).

The Banana Monument for Times Square [Plate 8] leads into the Fan. The Banana standing on my refrigerator demonstrated this: the transition was accomplished through an earlier design of Fan; it was a more modern Fan that had sort of a banana end. When you peel the banana, you get the four wings of the Fan (leaves). The Fan replaces the Statue of Liberty. This is to make you *feel* the large version of the object — i.e., *feel* the Fan the way one feels the Statue of Liberty. It's that heavy, that tall. There is a resemblance: the base of the Statue of Liberty is somewhat like a fan base; and she has this spiked ornament. You can also think of the Fan as sort of a substitute image of America. The suggestion is possibly there but I haven't drawn a conclusion. The Giant Fan was hung in the U. S. Pavilion at *Expo* in Montreal. "Fan" means Satan in Swedish — there is that area to explore. There is a black fan and a white one — a working of the theme of opposites in the context of superstition. I have a shiny black fan and a dry white fan — like the two angels, those winged victories that walk beside you — the white angel and the black angel. One for day, one for night; turn to the left, turn to the right. If people want to find things, they are probably there. I recently discovered that the windmill is the logos of New York City. There were once many, many fans on the hills around the bay.

Plate 36 (Monuments/71)
Proposed Colossal Monument for Central Park, NYC: Moving Pool Balls (1967).

Loose, the balls roll around and bump against the trees and the buildings at the side of the park. A more realistic thought would be to have them motorized like the gigantic, moving structures at Cape Kennedy. They could shift under control, so that everyday, as you got up in your apartment overlooking Central Park, the balls would be in a different position. They would be crawling all the time — all over Central Park. The effect is, of course, a pool table. The Balls would be different colors but not numbered. They would be hollow inside and could be used for housing or civic business. A whole Washington could be built this way. The positions would change all the time. It would be fun to have a constant movement of such houseballs back and forth across the whole U. S.

Plate 37 (Monuments/72)
Proposed Colossal Monument for Park Avenue, NYC: Bowling Balls (1967).

Looking down Park Avenue from 96th Street, I realized there was a gentle slope all the way down to the Grand Central Building. Looking up from Grand Central, I saw the stoplights in a row. That translated itself into the idea of balls rolling down the center of Park Avenue. They would roll down into a large portal arch in the Grand Central Building (certainly that grouping of buildings is one of the most violent and frightening in the world); then would be carried back underground via the railroad — an enlargement of the tunnels — to 96th Street again — the peak of the slope, and from there started down again — a constant flow of balls. They would be very large — 10, 12 stories high — red and green like the traffic lights. Or chrome to reflect the sides of the street as they rolled.

Proposed Colossal Monument for Grant Park, Chicago: Windshield Wiper (1967).

The Giant Wiper is an enormous blade attached to a housing on the spot of the now existent Buckingham (Bucky) Fountain in Grant Park. Being obsolete, the fountain is removed. The housing takes its place and twin rectangular pools are constructed extending south to Balbo Drive and north to Jackson Boulevard. These serve as swimming pools for the city's children. However, from time to time the blade of the Giant Wiper descends into the water. If one doesn't want to get hit, one must watch it and get out in time. The Wiper blade rises again and drips water from its hollow and absorbent parts almost until its perpendicular crest, then descends dry toward the pool opposite, to repeat the operation. A rainbow may be formed. The time of travel from one horizontal to the other may be adjusted. We start with fixing the time it takes a car to travel from Randolph Street to Roosevelt Road. On certain days, communities throughout the city may decide on a different pace. A button in the Art Institute will adjust it all. A frantic pace may be tried late at night. The Wiper may be illuminated in all colors. A solid fountain. The ice effects in winter will be marvelous, not to mention when the icicles break against the surface of the pools. If this monument proves to be impossible, I ask how then will architects honor their vow of instrumenting the imagination?

Plate 47 (Monuments/81)
Proposed Monument for the South-East Corner of North Avenue and Clark Street, Chicago: Bat Spinning at the Speed of Light (1967).

The Bat is a coneshaped metal form about the height of the former Plaza Hotel, placed with the narrower end down at the southeast corner of North Avenue and Clark Street. The Bat is kept spinning at an incredible speed — so fast it would burn one's fingers up the shoulders to touch it. However, the speed is invisible and to spectators the monument appears to be standing absolutely still.

Plate 46 (Buildings/7)

Late Submission to the Chicago Tribune Architectural Competition of 1922: Clothespin (1967).

In 1922, the *Chicago Tribune* conducted a competition for a new building which was won by the design that now stands. (The designs can be seen in: *The International Competition for a New Administration Building for the Chicago Tribune* (Chicago Tribune Company: 1923).) Among the designs submitted were several versions of a skyscraper in the form of a column, including one by Adolf Loos; a building in the form of an Indian with raised tomahawk; and another in the form of Skeezix, the comic strip character.

The "spring" of the Colossal Clothespin is a tunnel through which the wind can sound. The area between the "legs" would also be a huge wind tunnel, with blue glass facing the inside. The structure of the Clothespin echoes two recent Chicago buildings: the John Hancock Building and the First National Bank skyscraper. The rod of the spring along the side of the building would be glassed in and contain a restaurant.

Plate 48 (Monuments/85)

Proposed Colossal Monument to Replace the Washington Obelisk, Washington, D.C.:
Scissors in Motion (1967).

The handles of the monument are underground, balanced in great troughs which may be looked into. The handles are red. The blades part in the course of a day. At evening, the colossal red handles rise above the ground; they sink out of sight again when the sun sets. The closing continues slowly all night until dawn when the colossal blades are joined, forming a structure like the obelisk, catching the sun's light at the tips.

Plate 54 (Monuments/33)

Proposed Underground Memorial and Tomb for President John F. Kennedy (1965).

A hollow casting is made of the late President on the scale of the Statue of Liberty. The original is taken not from the man himself but from a photograph of the man, standing, his hands in his pockets, arms close to his body, legs together, figure stiff and erect. This gigantic casting is inserted head down into an excavation, and the earth closed around it. The shoe-bottoms are also covered so that the entire sculpture is invisible. An opening is left at the top about the size of a golf-hole, through which the interior of the sculpture may be seen by kneeling or lying on one's stomach. There is no other way to see the sculpture.

This hole is in the center of a square mile of grass carefully tended by an army of groundskeepers and bordered by trees. Nothing is visible on the surface except the men tending the grass and the line of sightseers waiting to peer down through the hole. The inside of the sculpture is brass, and here too a large staff is kept busy, polishing the sides by electric light, from scaffolds and suspended seats, like the window washers of sky-scrapers. The illuminated golden interior contrasts sharply with the green and bluish free space above the ground. From the top of the inverted sculpture — from the "soles" over the absent "shoes" — the sarcophagus may be hung by a long wire like a plastic mummy-case, head down in the posture of the colossal statue's invisible exterior, sway-ing slightly in a pendulum effect, responsive to the movement of the earth.

No Plate (Monument Models/14)
Proposal for the Louis Sullivan Tomb, Grant Park, Chicago.

The Sullivan Tomb is based on the anecdote that the architect spent the final years of his life sleeping on the floor of a small closet under a bare lightbulb. The Tomb is a huge brown structure. One enters by escalators that carry one from the ground up into a vast room which is very dark in contrast to the strong sunlight outside. One walks along the edge of the interior space and slowly becomes aware of the gigantic 600 foot lying figure of Sullivan in brown metal. It seems to be a mountain; it takes time to perceive that the rises and shapes are in the figure of a man. Upper parts are not easily visible except from a gallery near the ceiling which can be reached by elevators. A dim light emanates from an enormous lightbulb in the heights of the space. By its dim light one can barely make out the complex network of forms which cover the interior walls and ceil-ing like cobwebs — painstaking reproductions in metal and concrete of the Master's works.

The following two monuments exist as text only.

The Memorial to Baseball, Comiskey Park, Chicago.

Comiskey Park is shut down and completely restored. Enough white plaster figures in typical attitudes (five or six variations) are obtained to fill the stands, as on the Sunday of a vital series. Casts of the players are also made and placed in the position of playing ball. Visitors are strictly excluded, though color postcards are obtainable in front of the memorial. The monument is fairly visible from the air. The only person allowed inside is the groundskeeper. The grass is kept neat, healthy and green around the immovable figures.

The Memorial to Pinetop Smith, Chicago.

This is a wire strung westward over North Avenue (like the wire of the electric CTA bus) from Clark Street to the city limits or beyond. At intervals of 15 minutes, a blue impulse travels along the wire. In a split second, it moves from Clark to Austin Boulevard. Along its path, the impulse touches off a blue light at the intersection of Larrabee Street. Near there, according to legend, Pinetop Smith, the inventor of boogie woogie, was killed. The light burns about a minute and fades away. The monument ignites each evening at the same time as the city lights.

Oldenburg at the Lion's pedestal at the foot of Nelson's Column in Trafalgar Square, London, 1966

BIBLIOGRAPHY

Oldenburg looking at Nelson's Column in Trafalgar Square, London, 1966

Section I lists articles, introductions and notes by the artist containing statements about his "Proposals for Monuments and Buildings"; Section II, interviews with the artist in which he discussed the proposals; Section III, articles by others about the proposals. The items are listed chronologically.

I

STATEMENTS BY THE ARTIST

Remarks in the catalogue of the artist's show at Sidney Janis Gallery, New York, March 1966.

Remarks in "Claes Oldenburg, Sculpture and Drawings," catalogue of a retrospective show at the Moderna Museet, Stockholm, 1966. (Also contains "Project for a Solid Concrete War Memorial by Claes Oldenburg." Paper prepared for a class at Cornell University by students Evans, O'Brien and Schwartz.)

"Afterthoughts," *Konstrevy* (Stockholm), May 6, 1966.

"Some Program Notes about Monuments, Mainly," supplement to catalogue of the artist's show at the Sidney Janis Gallery, April 1967. This text was published in *Chelsea* #22-23, June 1968, 87-92.

Statement in *Perspecta 11* (Yale Architectural Journal), 1967, 52.

"America: War & Sex, Etc.," *Arts*, Summer 1967, 32ff.

Description of the Giant Windshield Wiper in *Panorama, Chicago Daily News,* July 22, 1967.

Notes on the Scissors Obelisk in portfolio commemorating the opening of the National Collection of Fine Arts, *List Poster Program,* published by H. K. L. Limited (Boston), 1967.

Notes and notebook specimens concerning the London Knees in boxed multiple "London Knees 1966," *Editions Alecto Ltd.,* (London/New York), 1968.

"Notes," twelve original color lithographs and text in folio, *Gemini G. E. L.* (Los Angeles), 1968.

"About the Famous Toronto Drainpipe," *Artscanada* (Toronto), August 1968, 40-41.

II

INTERVIEWS WITH THE ARTIST

Alfons Schilling, *Bau* (Vienna) #4, 1966, 83. Contains English translation in supplement.

Robert Fraser, "London: Male City," *International Times* (London), December 12-25, 1966.

Gene Baro, "Oldenburg's Monuments," *Art and Artists,* (London) December 1966, 28-31.

III

ARTICLES

Pierre Restany, "Claes Oldenburg 1965 e i desegni di 'Monumenti Giganti' per New York," *Domus* (Milan) 443, December 1965, 50-53.

Harris Rosenstein, "Climbing Mt. Oldenburg," *Art News,* February 1966, 21ff.

Öyvind Fahlström, "Object-making," translated introduction to the Stockholm catalogue, *Studio International* (London), December 1966, 328-329.

Gene Baro, "Claes Oldenburg, or The Things of This World," *Art International,* November 1966, 35ff.

Olle Granath, "How I Learned to Love the Tube: Reflections Surrounding a Stockholm Visitor," *Konstrevy* (Stockholm), May 6, 1966.

Jasia Reichardt, "Bridges and Oldenburg," *Studio International,* January 1967, 2-3.

Barrie Hale, "One Artist's Response to Toronto," *The Telegram* (Toronto), January 17, 1967.

Betty Flynn, "You Can Take an Object and Change it from Small to Big to Giant to Colossal," *Panorama, Chicago Daily News,* July 22, 1967, 2-3.

Dan Graham, "Oldenburg's Monuments," *Artforum,* January 1968, 30-39.

Jack Altman, "The Super, Giant, Economy-Sized Fantasies of the King of Neubern," *Midwest, Chicago Sun-Times,* February 18, 1968, 6-15.

CATALOGUE OF DRAWINGS OF PROPOSALS
FOR MONUMENTS AND BUILDINGS

Oldenburg measuring paving stones in Trafalgar Square, London, 1966

The entries are numbered in the sequence in which they were created, covering the period through May 1969.

I

MONUMENTS

1   *Proposed Colossal Monument for the Battery, NYC: Vacuum Cleaner (View from the Upper Bay).* 1965. Crayon and watercolor. 23 × 29 inches. Collection Jonathan Scull, New York.

2   *Proposed Colossal Monument for the Battery, NYC: Vacuum Cleaner (East River View).* 1965. Crayon and watercolor. 12 × 17¾ inches. Collection Mrs. Robert M. Benjamin, New York.

3   *Proposed Colossal Monument for the Battery, NYC: Vacuum Cleaner (View from Upper Bay).* 1965. Crayon and watercolor. 23 × 29 inches. Collection Jerry Spiegel, New York.

4   *Proposed Colossal Monument for Grand Army Plaza, NYC: Baked Potato.* 1965. Crayon and watercolor. 18 × 21½ inches. Collection Mr. and Mrs. Ira Licht, New York.

5   *Proposed Colossal Monument for Grand Army Plaza, NYC: Baked Potato (Thrown Version).* 1965. Crayon and watercolor. 23 × 29 inches. Thomas E. Benesch Memorial Collection, Baltimore Museum of Art.

6 *Proposed Colossal Monument for New York Harbor: Pizza for Upper Bay.* 1965. Crayon and watercolor. 12 × 18 inches. Collection Mr. and Mrs. Richard L. Selle, Chicago.

7 *Proposed Colossal Monument for New York Harbor: Pizza for Upper Bay.* 1965. Crayon and watercolor. 11¾ × 17½ inches. Collection Mr. and Mrs. Edwin Bergman, Chicago.

8 *Proposed Colossal Monument for New York Harbor: Pizza for Upper Bay (Scattered Slices).* 1965. Crayon and watercolor. 22¾ × 28¾ inches. Collection William Wixom, Cleveland.

9 *Proposed Monument for the Intersection of Canal Street and Broadway, NYC: Block of Concrete, Inscribed with the Names of War Heroes.* 1965. Crayon and watercolor. 11¾ × 17½ inches. Collection Mr. and Mrs. Daniel N. Flavin, Jr., Cold Spring, New York.

10 *Proposed Colossal Monument for Lower East Side, NYC: Ironing Board.* 1965. Crayon and watercolor. 21¾ × 29½ inches. Collection Mr. and Mrs. Marvin Goodman, Toronto.

11 *Proposed Colossal Monument for Lower East Side, NYC: Ironing Board.* 1965. Crayon and watercolor. 12 × 17¾ inches. Collection Louise Ferrari, Houston.

12 *Proposed Colossal Monument for Park Avenue, NYC: Good Humor Bar.* 1965. Crayon and watercolor. 12 × 17½ inches. Collection Mr. and Mrs. Dirk Lohan, Chicago.

13   *Proposed Colossal Monument for Times Square, NYC: Banana.* 1965. Crayon and watercolor. 11½ × 17½ inches. Collection Mr. and Mrs. Richard L. Selle, Chicago.

14   *Proposed Colossal Monument for Columbus Circle, NYC: Silex Juicit.* 1965. Crayon and watercolor. 29½ × 21½ inches. Collection Mr. and Mrs. Norman B. Champ Jr., St. Louis.

15   *Proposed Colossal Monument for Paterson, New Jersey: Cake Cover.* 1965. Crayon and watercolor. 18 × 23½ inches. Collection Mr. and Mrs. Jack Chasnoff, St. Louis.

16   *Proposed Colossal Monument for Central Park North, NYC: Teddy Bear.* 1965. Crayon and watercolor. 23 × 29 inches. Collection Alfred Heller, Grass Valley, California.

17   *Proposed Colossal Monument for Central Park North, NYC: Teddy Bear.* 1965. Crayon and watercolor. 23 × 30 inches. Collection William A. M. Burden, New York.

18   *Proposed Colossal Monument for Central Park North, NYC: Teddy Bear.* 1965. Crayon. Collection Mr. and Mrs. Carl E. Cassel, Essex Fells, New Jersey.

19   *Proposed Colossal Monument for New York Park: Teddy Bear (Thrown Version).* 1965. Crayon and watercolor. 23 × 29 inches. Collection Alfred Heller, Grass Valley, California.

20   *Proposed Colossal Monument for Times Square, NYC: Banana.* 1965. Crayon and watercolor. 12 × 17½ inches. Collection Mr. and Mrs. William Berman Jr., St. Louis.

21   *Proposed Colossal Monument for Times Square, NYC: Banana (all but the point of it behind the building).* 1965. Crayon and watercolor. 24 × 17½ inches. Collection Benjamin Dunkelman, Toronto.

22   *Proposed Colossal Monument for Staten Island, NYC: Fan (Study for cover of Domus Magazine—not used).* 1965. Crayon and watercolor. 23½ × 19 inches. Collection Mr. and Mrs. Richard E. Oldenburg, New York.

23   *Proposed Colossal Monument for Staten Island, NYC: Fan (Study for cover of Domus Magazine—not used).* 1965. Crayon and watercolor. 19 × 11½ inches. Collection D. and J. de Menil, Houston.

24   *Proposed Colossal Monument for Staten Island, NYC: Fan (Study for cover of Domus Magazine—not used).* 1965. Crayon and watercolor. 14½ × 11½ inches. Collection Mrs. S. Berland, Lawrence, Long Island, New York.

25   *Proposed Colossal Monument for Ellis Island: Frankfurter with Tomato and Toothpick.* 1965. Crayon and watercolor. 22 × 30 inches. Collection Mr. and Mrs. Michael Blankfort, Los Angeles.

26   *Proposed Colossal Monument for Ellis Island: Shrimp.* 1965. Crayon and watercolor. 12 × 15½ inches. Collection Mr. and Mrs. Dirk Lohan, Chicago.

27 *Proposed Monument for the Intersection of Canal Street and Broadway, NYC: Block of Concrete Inscribed with the Names of War Heroes*. 1965. Crayon and watercolor. 15⅞ × 12 inches. Collection Alicia Legg, New York.

28 *Proposed Colossal Monument for Central Park North, NYC: Teddy Bear*. 1965. Crayon and watercolor. 23 × 19 inches. Collection Mr. and Mrs. Richard E. Oldenburg, New York.

29 *Proposed Colossal Monument for Times Square, NYC: Banana*. 1965. Crayon and watercolor. 24½ × 19 inches. Collection Robert Fraser, London.

30 *Proposed Colossal Monument for Times Square, NYC: Banana*. 1965. Crayon and watercolor. 24 × 17½ inches. Private Collection, California.

31 *Proposed Colossal Monument for Park Avenue, NYC: Good Humor Bar*. 1965. Crayon and watercolor. 23½ × 17½ inches. Collection Carroll Janis, New York.

32 *Proposed Colossal Monument for Park Avenue, NYC: Good Humor Bar*. 1965. Crayon and watercolor. 16¾ × 13½ inches. Collection Mr. and Mrs. Michael Blankfort, Los Angeles.

33 *Proposed Underground Memorial and Tomb for President John F. Kennedy*. 1965. Spray paint on paper cut-out. 13¾ × 11 inches. Collection the Artist, New York.

34 *Proposed Monument for Karlaplan, Stockholm: Turning Wingnut*. 1966. Photoprint from pencil. 11⅝ × 16½ inches. Collection the Artist, New York.

35   *Proposed Colossal Monument Behind the Moderna Museet, Stockholm: Swedish Doorhandle and Locks, Two Views.* 1966. Pencil. 11⅝ × 16½ inches; 11¼ × 16½ inches. Collection the Artist, New York.

36   *Proposed Colossal Monument for Långholmen, Stockholm: Saw.* 1966.Pencil. Collection Archive of Decorative Art, Konsthall, Lund, Sweden.

37   *Proposed Monument for Långholmen, Stockholm: Stämpel (Office Stamp).* 1966. Crayon. Collection Archive of Decorative Art, Konsthall, Lund, Sweden.

38   *Proposed Colossal Monument for the Entrance to Stockholm Harbor: Pivoting Lion.* 1966. Crayon and watercolor. Collection K. G. Hulten, Stockholm.

39   *Proposed Colossal Monument for Piccadilly Circus: Pipe, Lighter and Valise.* 1966. Crayon and watercolor. 7½ × 9¼ inches. Collection Gudrun Osmond-Clark, London.

40   *Various Positions of a Giant Lipstick to Replace the Fountain of Eros, Piccadilly Circus.* 1966. Crayon and watercolor. 18 × 24 inches. Collection John and Kimiko Powers, Aspen, Colorado.

41   *Proposed Colossal Monument for Thames Estuary: Ear.* 1966. Crayon and watercolor. 7 × 9¾ inches. Stolen from Janis Gallery, April 1967.

42   *Proposed Colossal Monument for Thames Estuary: Knee.* 1966. Crayon and watercolor. 15¼ × 22⅛ inches. Collection D. and J. de Menil, Houston.

43 *Proposed Colossal Monument for Thames Estuary: Knee.* 1966. Crayon and water-color. 15 × 22 inches. Collection Mr. and Mrs. Dirk Lohan, Chicago.

44 *Proposed Colossal Monument for Thames Estuary: Knee.* 1966. Crayon and water-color. 15 × 22 inches. Collection Simone Withers Swann, New York.

45 *Proposed Colossal Monument to Replace the Nelson Column in Trafalgar Square: Gearstick in Motion.* 1966. Crayon and watercolor. 19 × 26 inches. Private Collection, New York.

46 *Proposed Colossal Monument to Replace the Nelson Column in Trafalgar Square: Gearstick in Motion.* 1966. Crayon and watercolor with magazine clipping. 15 × 22 inches. Collection Mr. and Mrs. Alfred Ordover, New York.

47 *Proposed Colossal Monument for Thames River: Thames Ball (View from Below).* 1966. Crayon and watercolor. 15 × 22 inches. Collection Neil Levine, New Haven.

48 *Thames Ball (Stages).* 1966. Crayon and watercolor. 15 × 22 inches. Collection Mr. and Mrs. M. Riklis, New York.

49 *Proposed Colossal Monument for Battersea Park: Drum Set.* 1966. Crayon and watercolor. 15 × 22 inches. Collection Mr. and Mrs. Edwin Bergman, Chicago.

50 *Fixture for a London Taxi: Interior Lamp in the Form of an Ear.* 1966. Crayon and watercolor. 21½ × 14½ inches. Collection Louise Ferrari, Houston.

51 *Small Study for Colossal Monument: Fagend.* 1966. Crayon and watercolor. 7 × 9¾ inches. Collection Mr. and Mrs. Ivan Karp, New York.

52 *Study for Colossal Monument: Fagends (in Hyde Park).* 1966. Crayon and watercolor. 15 × 22 inches. Collection Gordon Locksley Gallery, Minneapolis.

53 *Proposed Colossal Monument, Victoria Embankment, London: Knees.* 1966. Clipping on postcard: reproduced as giant postcard in "London Knees, 1966," multiple edition, Editions Alecto, London, 1968. 10 × 15¾ inches.

54 *Proposed Monument for Oslo: Frozen Ejaculation (Ski Jump).* 1966. Crayon and watercolor. 22 × 30 inches. Collection Mr. and Mrs. Dirk Lohan, Chicago.

55 *Proposal for Colossal Monuments: Lunch Box Contents on the Islands of the Upper Bay.* 1967. Crayon and watercolor. 26 × 40 inches.

56 *Proposed Colossal Monument for Toronto: Drainpipe.* 1967. Pencil and watercolor. 40 × 26 inches. Collection Joseph Kramer, Toronto.

57 *Proposed Colossal Monument for Toronto: Drainpipe.* 1967. Pencil and watercolor. 23 × 30 inches. Private Collection, Houston.

58 *Proposed Colossal Monument for Toronto: Drainpipe (View from Lake).* 1967. Crayon. 18 × 24 inches. Collection John and Kimiko Powers, Aspen, Colorado.

59 *Proposed Colossal Monument for Toronto: Drainpipe (View from the Air).* 1967. Crayon and watercolor. 22 × 30 inches.

60 *Base of Colossal Drainpipe Monument, Toronto, with Waterfall.* 1967. Pencil and watercolor. 24¾ × 22 inches. Collection John and Kimiko Powers, Aspen, Colorado.

61 *Base of Colossal Drainpipe Monument, Toronto: (Front View).* 1967. Ink and watercolor. 11 × 8½ inches. Collection Mr. and Mrs. Michael Blankfort, Los Angeles.

62 *Proposed Colossal Underground Monument, Toronto: Drainpipe.* 1967. Cutout, pencil, spray enamel and watercolor. 40 × 26 inches. Collection Mr. and Mrs. M. Riklis, New York.

63 *Proposed Colossal Underground Monument, Drainpipe.* 1967. Cutout, chalk, crayon, spray enamel and watercolor. 30 × 22 inches. Collection John and Kimiko Powers, Aspen, Colorado.

64 *"Capric"—Adapted to a Monument for a Park.* 1967. Crayon and watercolor. 22 × 30 inches. Collection John and Kimiko Powers, Aspen, Colorado.

65 *Small Monument for a London Street: Fallen Hat (For Adlai Stevenson).* 1967. Crayon. 15½ × 22 inches. Collection John and Kimiko Powers, Aspen, Colorado.

66 *Small Monument for a London Street: Fallen Hat (For Adlai Stevenson).* 1967. Pencil and watercolor. 23 × 32 inches. Collection John and Kimiko Powers, Aspen, Colorado.

67 *Proposed Colossal Monument for Thames River: Thames Ball.* 1967. Crayon, pen and watercolor on postcard. 3½ × 5½ inches. Collection Ed Janss, Thousand Oaks, California.

68 *Proposed Colossal Monument for Thames River: Thames Ball.* 1967. Crayon, pen and watercolor on postcard. 3½ × 5½ inches. Collection Carroll Janis, New York.

69 *Proposed Colossal Monument for Thames River: Thames Ball (View from River).* 1967. Pencil and watercolor. 26¼ × 40 inches. Collection Mr. and Mrs. R. H. Waddell, New York.

70 *Proposed Colossal Monument: Fan in Place of the Statue of Liberty.* 1967. Pencil. 26 × 40 inches. Collection Ondine Vaughn and Steve Schapiro, New York.

71 *Proposed Colossal Monument for Central Park, NYC: Moving Pool Balls.* 1967. Pencil and watercolor. 22 × 30 inches. Collection D. and J. de Menil, Houston.

72 *Proposed Colossal Monument for Park Avenue, NYC: Bowling Balls.* 1967. Pencil and watercolor. 27⅞ × 22¼ inches. Collection D. and J. de Menil, Houston.

73 *Colossal Fagend in Park Setting.* 1967. Pencil and watercolor. 30 × 22 inches. Collection Mrs. Christophe Thurman, New York.

74 *Colossal Fagends in Park Setting, with Man.* 1967. Pencil and watercolor. 30 × 22 inches. Collection Mrs. Rene d'Harnoncourt, New York.

75 *Colossal Fagends Installed on Doberman Estate, Westphalia, with Sheep-fagend Watching.* 1967. Pencil. 26 × 40 inches. Collection Mr. and Mrs. Richard L. Selle, Chicago.

76 *Proposed Monument to Commemorate Clarence Darrow: Typewriter Emerging from the Lagoon in Jackson Park, Chicago.* 1967. Crayon and watercolor. 16¾ × 16⅝ inches.

77 *Proposed Colossal Monument for Grant Park, Chicago: Windshield Wiper.* 1967. Crayon on postcards (3). Each 3½ × 5½ inches. Collection the Artist, New York.

78 *Proposed Colossal Monument for Grant Park, Chicago: Windshield Wiper (Overhead View).* 1967. Crayon and watercolor. 17 × 12½ inches. Collection Louise Ferrari, Houston.

79 *Proposed Colossal Monument for Grant Park, Chicago: Windshield Wiper (View from Lake).* 1967. Crayon and watercolor. 14 × 17 inches. Collection Mr. and Mrs. Richard L. Selle, Chicago.

80 *Proposed Colossal Monument for the West Side of Chicago in the Form of Smoke.* 1967. Crayon and watercolor. 7 × 9¾ inches. Collection the Artist, New York.

81 *Proposed Monument for the South-East Corner of North Avenue and Clark Street, Chicago: Bat Spinning at the Speed of Light.* 1967. Crayon and watercolor. 17¾ × 12 inches. Collection Frances and Sydney Lewis, Richmond, Virginia.

82 *Proposal for a Skyscraper in the Form of a Basketball Backstop, with Ball in Net.* 1967. Crayon and watercolor. 10⅝ × 7⅞ inches.

83 *Proposed Colossal Monument for the End of Navy Pier, Chicago: Side-view Mirror.* 1967. Crayon and watercolor. 7¾ × 10¼ inches.

84 *Proposed Colossal Monument for the End of Navy Pier, Chicago: Bed-table Lamp.* 1967. Crayon and watercolor. 13⅝ × 11 inches.

85 *Proposed Colossal Monument to Replace the Washington Obelisk, Washington, D.C.: Scissors in Motion.* 1967. Crayon and watercolor. 30 × 19¾ inches. Collection Philip Johnson, New Canaan, Connecticut.

86 *The Letter Q in Landscape.* 1968. Crayon and watercolor. 10½ × 13½ inches. Collection Caroline F. Solovei, New York.

87 *The Letters L and O in Landscape.* 1968. Crayon and watercolor. 9½ × 13½ inches. Collection John and Kimiko Powers, Aspen, Colorado.

88 *Inverted Nose in Landscape.* 1968. Crayon and watercolor. 7½ × 9½ inches. Private Collection, California.

89 *Inverted Nose in Landscape.* 1968. Crayon and watercolor. 7½ × 9½ inches. Collection John and Kimiko Powers, Aspen, Colorado.

90 *Proposed Colossal Monument for the End of Navy Pier, Chicago: Fireplug (Two Views).* 1968. Pencil. 30 × 22 inches.

91   *Study for a Colossal Monument to Mayor Daley #1*. 1968. Crayon. 11 × 13¾ inches.

92   *Study for a Colossal Monument to Mayor Daley #2*. 1968. Crayon. 11 × 13¾ inches.

II
BUILDINGS

1   *Terminus of Proposed New Bridge, Lidingö, Stockholm, in the Form of Swedish Bathtub Fixtures*. 1966. Crayon. Private Collection, Sweden.

2   *Beach House for East Hampton, Long Island in the Form of a Doorhandle*. 1967. Pencil. 22 × 30 inches. Collection Mr. Carter Burden, New York.

3   *Building in the Form of an English Extension Plug*. 1967. Pencil. 22 × 30 inches. Collection Mr. and Mrs. Arthur Cohen, New York.

4   *Proposed Chapel in the Form of Swedish Extension Plug*. 1967. Crayon and watercolor. 22 × 30 inches. Collection Krannert Art Museum, Champaign, Illinois.

5   *Late Submission to the Chicago Tribune Architectural Competition of 1922: Perpendicular Ore Boat*. 1967. Crayon and watercolor. 9¾ × 7 inches. Private Collection, Houston.

6   *Late Submission to the Chicago Tribune Architectural Competition of 1922: Clothespin (Version One)*. 1967. Pencil, crayon and watercolor. 22 × 23¼ inches. Collection Philip Johnson, New Canaan, Connecticut.

7 *Late Submission to the Chicago Tribune Architectural Competition of 1922: Clothespin (Version Two)*. 1967. Pencil, crayon and watercolor. 22 × 23¼ inches. Collection Charles Cowles, New York.

8 *Design for a Police Building Using the Word POLICE*. 1968. Pencil. 22 × 30 inches. Collection John and Kimiko Powers, Aspen, Colorado.

9 *Museum Design Based on a Cigarette Package*. 1968. Pencil. 22 × 30 inches. Collection Irving Blum, Los Angeles.

10 *Design for a Bowling Alley in the Form of a Cigarette and Smoke*. 1968. Crayon and watercolor. 22 × 30 inches. Collection Mr. and Mrs. Roger Davidson, Toronto.

11 *Design for a Tunnel Entrance in the Form of a Nose*. 1968. Crayon. 22 × 30 inches. Collection Irving Blum, Los Angeles.

12 *Design for a Tunnel Entrance in the Form of a Nose*. 1968. Crayon and watercolor. 9½ × 7½ inches. Private Collection, California.

13 *Design for a Tunnel Entrance in the Form of a Nose*. 1968. Crayon and watercolor. 7½ × 9½ inches. Collection John and Kimiko Powers, Aspen, Colorado.

14 *Proposal for a Skyscraper in the Form of a Chicago Fireplug*. 1968. Crayon and watercolor. 13¾ × 11 inches.

15 *Proposal for a Tomb in the Form of a Giant Punching Bag*. 1968. Crayon. 11 × 13¾ inches.

16 *Proposal for a Tomb in the Form of a Giant Punching Bag—With Obelisk.* 1968. Crayon. 11 × 13¾ inches.

17 *Proposal for a Skyscraper in the Form of a Chicago Fireplug—Inverted Version.* 1969. Crayon and watercolor. 17¾ × 12 inches.

18 *Proposal for a Skyscraper for Michigan Avenue, Chicago, in the Form of Lorado Taft's Sculpture "Death."* 1968. Pen and pencil on postcard and clipping. 11¾ × 9¾ inches. Collection the Artist, New York.

III

MONUMENT MODELS

The following are three-dimensional scale models for monuments. Among them are models for "feasible monuments." The term feasible monuments is used by the artist to distinguish those proposals which were made with a deliberate consideration of scale, materials, and sites possible and available under present conditions: that is, monuments which *could* be built now. These are distinct from the proposals labeled "colossal," which are for monuments which cannot be built under present limitations, but can only be imagined.

1 *Model for a Colossal Monument: Wingnut (Stockholm).* 1966-67. Wood and liquitex. 36½ × 42¼ × 52¼ inches. Collection Mr. and Mrs. C. Bagley Wright, Seattle.

2   *Model for a Colossal Monument: Row of Bitten Knackebrod (Stockholm).* 1966. Knackebrod, cardboard, wood, watercolor. Collection the Artist, New York.

3   *Model for a Colossal Monument: Door Handle and Locks (Stockholm).* 1966-67. Wood, cardboard, liquitex. 6½ × 30 × 40 inches. Collection the Artist, New York.

4   *Prototype of Thames Ball.* 1967. Toilet float, plaster, liquitex. 4 × 5 × 16 inches.

5   *Model for a Colossal Monument: Thames Ball (London).* 1967. Wood and liquitex. 16½ × 42¼ × 52¼ inches. Collection Mr. and Mrs. Roger Davidson, Toronto.

6   *Model for a Colossal Monument: Drainpipe (Toronto).* 1967. Wood and liquitex. 64 × 33 × 17 inches. Collection Dr. Peter Ludwig, Aachen, W. Germany.

7   *Model for a Giant Traveling and Telescoping Lipstick, With Changeable Parts Showing Three Stages of Extension.* 1969. Cardboard and fabric, painted and shellacked.
    Tractor: 5⅝ × 16¼ × 25 inches.
    Stage 1: 4 × 8½ × 10¼ inches.
    Stage 2: 14½ × 8½ × 10¼ inches.
    Stage 3: 23½ × 8½ × 10¼ inches.

8   *Model for a Giant Tube Being Stepped On.* 1969. Cardboard and fabric, painted and shellacked. 15½ × 18½ × 13 inches. On cardboard base (by Artist). 4⅝ × 11¼ × 18¾ inches.

9   *Model for a Giant Ice Bag on a Corner Site.* 1969. Cardboard and fabric, painted and shellacked. 9 × 29 × 34 inches.

10 *Feasible Monument for a City Square: Hats Blowing in the Wind.* 1969. Cardboard and fabric, painted and shellacked. 10½ × 28 × 39 inches.

11 *Feasible Monument for a Tomb in the Form of a Punching Bag.* 1969. Cardboard and fabric, painted and shellacked. 18¾ × 28 × 36 inches.

12 *Feasible Monument for a Chicago Site: Fragment of the Older City (Old Town Monument).* 1969. Cardboard, painted and shellacked. 17 × 14⅛ × 20¼ inches.

13 *Feasible Monument for a Chicago Site: Giant Cuff-Link Using Picasso Head.* 1969. Cardboard, painted and shellacked. 14 × 23½ × 27 inches.

14 *Feasible Monument for Grant Park, Chicago: Memorial to Louis Sullivan.* 1969. Cardboard, painted and shellacked. 14 × 23½ × 27 inches.

15 *Feasible Monuments to be Scattered in a City Park: Fragments of Nightstick Contact.* 1968-69. Plaster, fabric, cardboard, painted, in 5 boxes filled with dirt. Each box: 2½ × 10 × 12 inches. Sample dimensions: 1¾ × 7 × 10 inches.

IV
EXECUTED MONUMENTS

This is the only monument realized so far, echoing the use of newspaper clippings mentioned in the interview.

1 *Pop Tart.* On Wall of Building Directly East of Museum of Contemporary Art, Ontario Street, Chicago. First version, October 1967. Replaced May 1969. Wall painting commissioned by the Museum, executed from a clipping supplied by the artist from a Chicago newspaper. 22 × 15½ feet.